The Nonprofit
Dashboard
A Tool for Tracking Progress

by Lawrence M. Butler

BOARDSOURCE®
Building Effective Nonprofit Boards

Library of Congress Cataloging-in-Publication Data

Butler, Lawrence, 1942-.

    The nonprofit dashboard: a tool for tracking progress / by Lawrence Butler.

        p. cm.

    An accompanying CD-ROM includes dashboard generator files, using Microsoft Excel, with templates for creating customizable dashboards for reporting.

ISBN 1-58686-097-6 (pbk.)

1. Nonprofit organizations—Evaluation. 2. Organizational effectiveness—Measurement.
3. Performance—Measurement. 4. Dashboards (Management information systems) I. Title.

HD62.6.B88 2007

658.4'01—dc22

                    2006038342

© 2007 BoardSource.
First printing, January 2007.
ISBN 1-58686-097-6

Published by BoardSource
1828 L Street, NW, Suite 900
Washington, DC 20036

The Nonprofit Dashboard: A Tool for Tracking Progress was made possible in part by the MetLife Foundation.

Building Effective Nonprofit Boards

Formerly the National Center for Nonprofit Boards

BoardSource, formerly the National Center for Nonprofit Boards, is the premier resource for practical information, tools and best practices, training, and leadership development for board members of nonprofit organizations worldwide. Through our highly acclaimed programs and services, BoardSource enables organizations to fulfill their missions by helping build strong and effective nonprofit boards.

BoardSource provides assistance and resources to nonprofit leaders through workshops, training, and our extensive Web site, www.boardsource.org. A team of BoardSource governance consultants works directly with nonprofit leaders to design specialized solutions to meet organizations' needs and assists nongovernmental organizations around the world through partnerships and capacity building. As the world's largest, most comprehensive publisher of materials on nonprofit governance, BoardSource offers a wide selection of books, videotapes, CDs, and online tools. BoardSource also hosts the BoardSource Leadership Forum, bringing together governance experts, board members, and chief executives of nonprofit organizations from around the world.

Created out of the nonprofit sector's critical need for governance guidance and expertise, BoardSource is a 501(c)(3) nonprofit organization that has provided practical solutions to nonprofit organizations of all sizes in diverse communities. In 2001, BoardSource changed its name from the National Center for Nonprofit Boards to better reflect its mission. Today, BoardSource has approximately 11,000 members and has served more than 75,000 nonprofit leaders.

For more information, please visit our Web site, www.boardsource.org, e-mail us at mail@boardsource.org, or call us at 800-883-6262.

Have You Used These BoardSource Resources?

VIDEOS

Meeting the Challenge: An Orientation to Nonprofit Board Service

Speaking of Money: A Guide to Fundraising for Nonprofit Board Members

BOOKS

The Board Chair Handbook

Managing Conflicts of Interest: A Primer for Nonprofit Boards

Driving Strategic Planning: A Nonprofit Executive's Guide

Taming the Troublesome Board Member

Presenting: Board Orientation

Presenting: Nonprofit Financials

Meet Smarter: A Guide to Better Nonprofit Board Meetings

The Board Building Cycle: Nine Steps to Finding, Recruiting, and Engaging Nonprofit Board Members

The Nonprofit Policy Sampler, Second Edition

The Source: Twelve Principles of Governance That Power Exceptional Boards

Nonprofit Board Answer Book: Practical Guide for Board Members and Chief Executives

The Nonprofit Legal Landscape

Self-Assessment for Nonprofit Governing Boards

Assessment of the Chief Executive

Fearless Fundraising

The Nonprofit Board's Guide to Bylaws

Understanding Nonprofit Financial Statements

Transforming Board Structure: Strategies for Committees and Task Forces

THE GOVERNANCE SERIES

1. *Ten Basic Responsibilities of Nonprofit Boards*
2. *Financial Responsibilities of Nonprofit Boards*
3. *Structures and Practices of Nonprofit Boards*
4. *Fundraising Responsibilities of Nonprofit Boards*
5. *Legal Responsibilities of Nonprofit Boards*
6. *The Nonprofit Board's Role in Setting and Advancing the Mission*
7. *The Nonprofit Board's Role in Planning and Evaluation*
8. *How To Help Your Board Govern More and Manage Less*
9. *Leadership Roles in Nonprofit Governance*

For an up-to-date list of publications and information about current prices, membership, and other services, please call BoardSource at 800-883-6262 or visit our Web site at www.boardsource.org.

Contents

Introduction

It's been said that "if you don't know where you're going, any road will take you there." But knowing the destination — even having a road map — while essential, is not enough. What if there were no road signs, speed and fuel gauges, and warning light indicators? No external signals to indicate progress along a chosen path and internal signals to keep the driver aware of the vehicle's speed, condition, and performance?

Like the instrument panel on the dashboard of an automobile, dashboard reports present a quick, comprehensible overview of an organization's status and overall direction. Instead of speed, RPM, and engine temperature, the dashboard typically displays preselected, critical measures of organizational performance and mission effectiveness. With dashboard reports that present key indicators in consistent formats, board members can readily spot changes and trends in these measurements. And like the dashboard inside a car, these reports often display the equivalent of warning lights that only flare up when there is an impending problem or when certain variables stray outside of predetermined limits.

Ultimately, dashboard metrics convey the big picture and yet are sensitive to both negative and positive changes in performance. The dashboard serves as an early warning device alerting the board and senior staff when it might be important to dig deeper for greater insight.

WHY CREATE A DASHBOARD?

Board members and senior staff may wonder why they need another report adding to the already overwhelming array of documents disseminated to the board in thick meeting binders, attached to e-mail messages, and on Web sites or intranets. What does a dashboard report give them that any number of other reporting formats doesn't already accomplish?

The answer, of course, is that governing boards *do not* need more reports or more information. What they do need is more meaning — and the dashboard report is one practical tool for conveying meaning directly and succinctly to hard-pressed board members. The dashboard report helps nonprofit leaders focus their attention on what matters most in their organizations, and, in doing so, gain greater insight and ascribe greater meaning to other available data. The learning opportunities gained from defining key performance indicators and tracking, reviewing, and evaluating them allow nonprofit leaders to improve and further fulfill the mission of their organizations. Learning is the major driver for this kind of information — why do it if not to learn from it, act upon it, and, ultimately, make better decisions about the organization's future?

At a time when governance has come under increased scrutiny by the media, regulatory agencies, and the public at large, the board's ability to quickly access critical outcome and performance information is being encouraged as never before.

More and more, the board's information resources are being viewed as vital to effective governance — from general oversight and monitoring of performance to making strategic decisions and raising red flags. And yet, board members claim that as they receive more data than they can handle, they continue to receive less meaningful information.

Dashboards also provide a great opportunity for partnership between board and staff. Creating these reports is largely a staff-driven process in support of the board's oversight role. The reports themselves help in maintaining both staff accountability and board focus on overall organizational performance rather than operational detail.

ABOUT THE BOOK

Chapters 1 and 2 address boards that are interested in making dashboards part of a regular board reporting process. These chapters provide board members with the framework for how dashboards fit into the context of effective governance practices, discuss how information is shared with the board, and help the board (along with senior staff) define the kind of information that will be represented in the report. Chapters 3 and 4 are intended to help staff with the nuts and bolts of designing dashboard reports and describe the process board and staff may undertake to develop an ongoing dashboard program. Chapter 5 discusses how dashboards are used in the context of board meetings and decision making.

Remember: No two organizations are exactly alike. The information an organization chooses to display in a dashboard should be reflective of its strategic plan, goals, and mission. Each organization that undertakes this process needs to pick and choose the key indicators, report design format, and board-staff collaboration process that works best for its particular circumstances. This book is not intended to be a one-size-fits-all instruction book that gives a nonprofit an exact blueprint for developing, designing, and maintaining a dashboard reporting system. It does, however, present the options, offer detailed illustrations and considerations, and provide a template from which to start.

USING THE CD-ROM

To help organizations get started with their own dashboard reports, the accompanying CD-ROM includes dashboard generator files, using Microsoft® Excel, with templates for creating customizable dashboards and how-to instructions for working with the files (see Chapter 5 for more guidance).

Also included on the CD-ROM is a board information survey for creating a baseline assessment of how the board views the kind of information it currently receives and the way in which it receives it. The information gathered is intended to help staff identify how it can communicate more effectively with the board and assist in developing the dashboard (see Chapter 4 for more detail).

1.
Understanding the Big Picture

Dashboards, like any report format, are limited in what they can accomplish. To provide meaning and insight, a dashboard report needs to be understood and used within the context of organizational planning and evaluation.

RESULTS-ORIENTED GOVERNANCE

In the BoardSource book *The Source: Twelve Principles of Governance That Power Exceptional Boards*, Principle 9 states: "Exceptional boards are results-oriented. They measure the organization's advancement towards mission and evaluate the performance of major programs and services."[1]

The book continues on to say that while most responsible boards monitor organizational performance by reviewing year-end financial reports and programmatic progress, truly exceptional boards measure overall efficiency, effectiveness, and impact. Board and staff need to agree on critical indicators that flow from the organization's mission, vision, and strategic priorities in addition to consideration of the community's needs, the work of comparable organizations, and the organization's operating environment. Exceptional boards routinely monitor progress by investing in the thoughtful development of key indicators and in the organizational infrastructure to report on them. Together, board and staff use these indicators to identify early successes so they may be maximized and potential problems so they can be addressed before they escalate.

Boards that intend to introduce improvements to governance information are encouraged to first take a hard look at all aspects of board performance and to make sure that the ground in which information seeds are planted is hospitable soil. No matter how well dashboard reports or any other information regularly given to the board is designed, if board members don't show up for meetings or the meetings are run inefficiently, the benefits of enhanced information will be lost. Effective governance begins with board discipline.

PLANNING AND EVALUATING: WHERE DOES A DASHBOARD FIT IN?

In *The Nonprofit Board's Role in Planning and Evaluation*, the connection between strategic planning and evaluation is very clear:

> Strategic planning allows the board to measure whether (or the extent to which) the organization has been effective in accomplishing its mission.

---

1. *The Source: Twelve Principles of Governance That Power Exceptional Boards.* Washington, DC: BoardSource, 2005.

It offers a road map and benchmarks to measure organizational effectiveness because the performance measurements identified through strategic planning are key indicators of organizational performance.[2]

The authors go on to note that "many organizations do not include performance measures or evaluative components in their strategic plans, but some choose to do so to enhance the organization's ability to successfully implement the plan." For each strategic goal and accompanying objectives, the authors emphasize that the organization needs to define what success would look like if they were achieved. "A strategic plan ultimately determines the design of an organization's performance measures."

Figure 1 below, adapted from this book, portrays the ongoing, alternating sequence of planning and evaluation in the assessment of organizational effectiveness over time. Performance measurement is essential for each round of evaluation to take place. And it is within this performance measurement module that dashboards reside. Here, dashboard reporting can be seen as an integral part of the cycle of organizational or program evaluation and assessment.

WHAT ARE DASHBOARD REPORTS?

Dashboards are really nothing more than user-friendly tools for displaying performance measures. These measures, whether in the form of indicators, variables, or ratios, are not the end product of organizational or program evaluation but the top

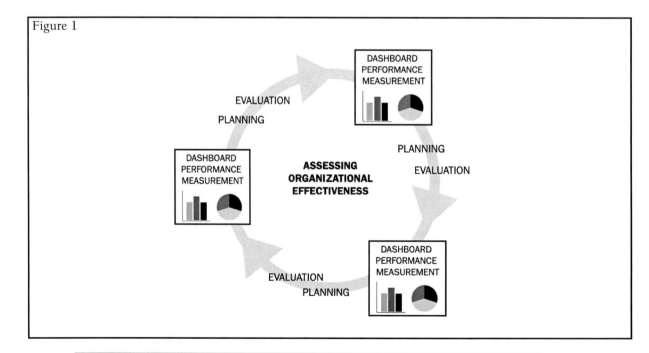

Figure 1

2. Yankey, John A. and Amy McClellan. *The Nonprofit Board's Role in Planning and Evaluation.* Washington, DC: BoardSource, 2003.

layer — the high-level view that points board and staff to where they might need to drill down into a more detailed, refined understanding of organizational and program effectiveness. They provide a learning opportunity for both board and staff: What is working well? What went wrong? How can the organization improve and further fulfill its mission? Dashboards are not only a powerful tool for staff to communicate important information to the board, but also for alerting staff to internal or external changes that could affect the way programs are administered.

Again, dashboards contain several key indicators of organizational performance: measures that demonstrate progress toward a goal and warning lights that only turn on when there is a pending problem. This latter feature allows the board to ignore a great deal of operational information, knowing that it will be alerted if a problem arises that requires attention.

WHAT AND HOW IS THE INFORMATION DISPLAYED?

In addition to key indicators and warning lights, dashboard reports can contain items that meet specific organizational needs. For example, if a nonprofit is undergoing a period of rapid development, the dashboard report might deliver information on the status of strategic initiatives designed to produce orderly growth. Key indicators might be reported to reflect the impact of these initiatives (e.g., new revenues resulting from those initiatives versus revenues from "traditional" business). Similarly, if the organization is facing a problem that threatens its survival, there may be specific indicators to reflect the status of that problem and the efforts directed at managing it. These special items can be added to the dashboard when the board feels it necessary, and eliminated when they are no longer relevant.

Service volume indicators are also common to dashboard reporting. These can be expressed in terms of the number of clients served or traditional units of services, such as patient days in a hospital, visits to a homeless shelter, or daycare enrollments.

In certain cases, the use of narrative can add real value to the dashboard's charts and graphs. In the absence of more structured qualitative data, anecdotes and stories can help to round out the board's understanding and to put into words what the numbers may not be able to fully communicate. Often by using stories, the board can better understand what impact the organization's mission is having or put into perspective why the continuation of an organization's program is still so very important.

For organizations just starting out or those that have yet to embark on more sophisticated data collection, many of the key indicators may not yet be available to track, compile, and display. Instead, some organizations may chart more basic information such as year-to-date fundraising results, new member enrollment, or basic financial data. Others may prefer to start out by choosing one or two key indicators and then gradually incorporate new indicators throughout the year or over the course of several years. By keeping the information simple, board members can focus on what is important to know without becoming overwhelmed with information that may distract them from the work at hand.

PRESENTING DATA IN CONSISTENT FORMATS

When a board becomes accustomed to seeing data in the same format over time, it is easier to spot patterns of change and problems that pose concern. This is not to say that, over time, the format for these reports cannot vary. Some evolution is certainly desirable and necessary as new issues arise and different indicators require monitoring. Some variation might also be deliberate. For example, a dashboard might combine some displays that are the same at each board meeting with other displays that appear in a rotating sequence over the course of a year's board meetings in order to expose the board to a broader range of information.

Consistency in the coding schemes used in dashboards and other reports — the positioning of graphic elements, the meaning of different colors or shading patterns, the terms in which numerical values are expressed, etc. — enable users to decipher the data more efficiently and thus allow them to spend their time thinking about meaning and significance rather than basic comprehension.

The same concern about consistent usage should apply to terms of reference, names, and acronyms. Staff, being closer to the day-to-day activities of the organization, are more accustomed to variations in terminology and usage, but board members, whose involvement can be more sporadic, may became thoroughly confused — even alienated — by such changes.

BASIC STYLES OF DASHBOARD REPORTING

The style of dashboard reporting that is most recognizable to those familiar with the evolution of this concept in the for-profit sector (popularized by techniques such as the Balanced Scorecard[3]) has become increasingly common in nonprofits, especially in health care institutions where there has long been an awareness of the need to monitor critical variables that have an impact on patient health outcomes.

Figure 2 is an example of a dashboard of this kind. In this case, the board of a hospital receives a quarterly report that summarizes on a single page 40 key performance indicators. The actual year-to-date numbers are presented for each indicator along with predetermined goals or targets and the resulting variances between actual and targeted performance. By scanning the color-coded icons (also signified by shape so that black and white copies of a color-coded report can still be interpreted), the user is able to quickly spot where the hospital is performing positively in relation to the goal (green arrow pointing up), not so well (red arrow pointing down), or where there is some possible early indication of negative performance (yellow diamond).

What is important to note about this summary or "scorecard" style of dashboarding is the high degree of analytical insight required to produce the report. Senior management and the board will have already determined which key performance indicators to measure, along with a desired level of performance in each case. These performance goals or targets are often referred to as benchmarks and they can be

---

3. *See* Kaplan, Robert S. and David P. Norton. "The Balanced Scorecard: Measures That Drive Performance." *Harvard Business Review*. July 2005.

Figure 2

SAMPLE MEDICAL CENTER
BOARD OF TRUSTEES QUARTERLY DASHBOARD
Year to Date / Second Quarter 2006

	INDICATOR		ACTUAL	GOAL/TARGET	VARIANCE	COMPARISON
	FINANCE				( ) = UNFAVORABLE	
1	ADJUSTED DISCHARGES	◇	5,184	5,236	(52)	BUDGET
2	CONTROLLABLE COST PER ADJ. DISCHARGE (CMA)*	▲	$ 3,824	$ 3,905	$ 81	BUDGET
3	NET PATIENT REVENUE PER ADJ. DISCHARGE	▲	$ 6,451	$ 6,124	$ 327	BUDGET
4	NET INCOME	▲	$ 3,315,979	$ 2,381,115	$ 934,864	BUDGET
5	CORE EARNINGS	▼	$ 1,080,177	$ 1,280,667	($200,490)	BUDGET
6	DAYS IN ACCOUNTS RECEIVABLE	▼	63.30	58.02	(5.28)	BUDGET
7	DAYS CASH ON HAND	▲	384.65	225.39	159.26	BUDGET
8	SUPPLY EXPENSE PER ADJ. DISCHARGE (CMA)*	▲	$ 918	$ 927	$9	BUDGET
	* CMA + Case Mix Adjusted					
	VOLUMES					
9	INPATIENT ACUTE ADMISSIONS	◇	3,378	3,447	(69)	BUDGET
10	TCU ADMISSIONS	▼	113	120	(7)	BUDGET
11	OUTPATIENT VISITS (INCLUDES OB)	▲	12,920	12,307	613	BUDGET
12	EMERGENCY ROOM VISITS	▲	8,922	8,100	822	BUDGET
13	INPATIENT SURGERY	▲	1,083	1,055	28	BUDGET
14	OUTPATIENT SURGERY	▲	1,423	1,234	189	BUDGET
15	HOME HEALTH VISITS	▲	13,864	11,400	2,464	BUDGET
	CUSTOMER SATISFACTION					
16	WILLING TO RETURN	◇	93.0%	95.1%	-2.1%	PRIOR YEAR
17	WILLING TO RECOMMEND	◇	91.9%	94.1%	-2.2%	PRIOR YEAR
18	QUALITY INDEX SCORE	◇	4.25	4.28	(0.03)	PRIOR YEAR
19	WAITING TIME REGISTRATION	▲	80.3%	80.0%	0.3%	LESS THAN 10 MIN.
20	EMPL. MORE CONCERNED WITH PATIENT THAN SELVES	◇	4.23	4.29	(0.06)	PRIOR YEAR
	CLINICAL OUTCOME					
21	C-SECTION RATE	▲	20.1	22.7	2.6	STATE DEP. HEALTH
22	NOSOCOMIAL INFECTION RATE	▲	3.05	3.15	0.10	PRIOR YEAR
23	NUMBER OF DEATHS / 1000 DISCHARGES	▼	35	32	(3)	PRIOR YEAR
24	FALL RATE / 1000 PATIENT DAYS	▼	4.03	3.23	(0.80)	PRIOR YEAR
25	MEDICATION ERRORS / 1000 PATIENT DAYS	▲	2.01	2.76	0.75	PRIOR YEAR
	UTILIZATION					
26	ACUTE LOS (ALL PAYORS)	▲	5.14	5.19	0.05	BUDGET
27	ACUTE LOS (MEDICARE)	◇	6.62	6.59	(0.03)	BUDGET
28	TCU LOS (ALL PAYORS)	▲	12.98	20.00	7.02	BUDGET
29	DRG 106 LOS (ALL PAYORS)	▼	11.92	10.16	(1.76)	TARGET
30	DRG 107 LOS (ALL PAYORS)	▲	6.54	6.87	0.33	TARGET
	SAFETY/RISK MANAGEMENT					
31	PATIENT OCCURRENCE REPORTS	▼	239	143	(96)	PRIOR YEAR
32	VISITOR OCCURRENCE REPORTS	▼	7	2	(5)	PRIOR YEAR
33	EMPLOYEE INJURIES	▲	59	145	86	PRIOR YEAR
34	DAYS LOST	▲	9	148	139	PRIOR YEAR
35	WORKERS COMP. CLAIMS	▲	9	26	17	PRIOR YEAR
	MANAGED CARE					
36	COVERED LIVES	▼	3,987	5,339	(1,352)	BUDGET
37	PHO NET INCOME (LOSS)	▼	($395,104)	$ 0	($395,104)	BUDGET
	HUMAN RESOURCES					
38	EMPLOYEE TURNOVER RATE	▲	4.0%	4.9%	0.9%	HEALTHCARE ADVISORY
	ETHICS					
39	NUMBER OF ETHICS EDUCATION PROGRAMS	▲	1	1	–	ASI STANDARD
40	NUMBER OF ETHICS COMMITTEE MEETINGS	▲	5	3	2	ASI STANDARD

▲ ON OR AHEAD OF TARGET   ◇ 1–5% BELOW TARGET   ▼ >5% BELOW TARGET

externally derived — an industry norm or standard, for example — or a "best practice" performance level achieved by peer institutions. Or, they can take the form of internal benchmarks based on the organization's own historical performance, budget projections, or mission-based aspirations.

Armed with this depth of prior understanding, a board member can quickly review the report and know which aspects of organizational performance are under control and which others require deeper analysis or probing. The summary dashboard is a powerful data presentation format not only because it employs compelling, visual metaphors (like traffic-light colors, arrows, meters, and gauges) to direct the viewer's attention to the critical issues, but also because it rests upon this foundation of prior analytical and collaborative effort.

Another more graphically oriented style of dashboard reporting is illustrated by Figure 3. This one-page report was designed to meet the needs of an art museum board. It combines graphic displays with numbers and brief narrative comments. At first glance, this report seems quite complex — a lot of numerical and graphic information is communicated on a single page. Looking at each window individually reveals multiple perspectives on the institution's progress. Combining them on the same page enables the viewer to see connections among these various perspectives.

Window 1 compares actual year-to-date revenues to the current and previous years' budgets in a graphic form similar to museum revenues by source as shown in window 3. Window 2 provides numerical details for windows 1 and 3, combining graphic and numerical terms to communicate with board members who have different preferences for receiving information.

Since this museum is interested in expanding revenues from public support, this is examined further in other windows. Window 5 shows membership trends over the past two years and window 6 breaks down the sources of public support. The placement of window 4 (with its monthly display of cumulative income versus budgeted income) above window 7 (which shows the monthly visits this year versus the average of the past two years) permits the eye to spot relationships between attendance levels and income.

Throughout this dashboard report there is an attempt to provide comparisons — actual versus budget, this year versus last year. These and other comparisons give the board a context for extracting meaning from the data. The window on the lower right is reserved for words highlighting and explaining key points revealed by the data. Each point is bulleted with the window number it refers to.

Of these two basic styles of dashboard reporting, the summary approach (Figure 2) works well not only in hard copy but online where the color-coded icons can be used as hyperlinks that, when clicked, allow the user to jump to another page with greater explanatory detail. The graphic style (Figure 3) with its multiple charts, numbers, and words arranged on a single page tends to work better in hard copy. Online versions of such dashboards often require scrolling to clearly see all the detail, which can offset the user's ability to take in the entire page at a glance and spot patterns of change. Whatever style of dashboard — be it a summary (or scorecard) dashboard, a graphic dashboard, or some combination — they share the basic principle of combining a set of well-chosen indicators of organizational performance and impact that quickly conveys meaning.

Figure 3

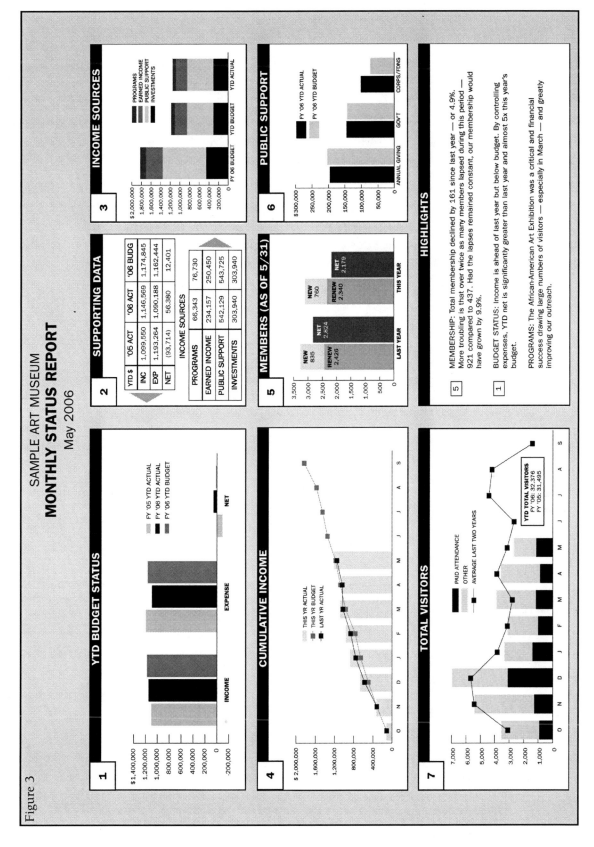

Incorporating Dashboards into Overall Board Communications

As compelling and useful as they are, dashboard reports represent only one component in an array of information resources available to a governing board. And, it is important to note that dashboard reports should not be substituted for more detailed reporting formats, auditor's reports, studies, and databases. The dashboard is just one of the tools for staff to better communicate with the board and prompt further board discussions.

Meeting minutes, budgets, financial statements, issue papers, and staff presentations are among other important pieces of a total system of governance information. All of these pieces can be enhanced through dashboard formatting. For example, a traditional line-item budget might still be provided in the board's meeting book, but its major implications can be summarized using a brief set of narrative points or graphic displays in dashboard form. This summary material could appear in the meeting book to convey the most significant information before the reader is confronted with the backup detail.

Additional reading materials — articles, extracted text, Web sites — can be provided to supplement those dashboards that reveal significant changes or trends. The chief executive can weigh in with explanation in a letter or presentation at a board meeting. Other experts from within or outside the organization can be invited to address the board on the significance of particular trends or noteworthy changes.

A comprehensive system of board information might comprise the following components:

- **Dashboard Reports**

   Typically limited to one or two pages, this report format assists the board in quickly assessing the status of the organization. Dashboards present selected key indicators in formats that are consistent from meeting to meeting.

- **Committee Reports**

   These reports document the activities and issues covered by board committees. By treating issues in greater depth, committee reports can often yield insights that might not surface in a dashboard report.

- **Meeting Book**

   Dashboard and committee reports are among the set of materials contained in the packet of information sent out to the board prior to each board meeting. With some good organization, this packet can help facilitate the board members' access to and understanding of the information needed for effective meeting participation.

- **Board Member Handbook**

   Typically, the handbook is a separate, loose-leaf binder containing background information on the organization that tends not to change from meeting to meeting (e.g., mission and values statements, strategic plan, executive bios). The handbook should be regularly updated and provide board members with a ready reference guide and orientation manual.

- **Chief Executive's Report**

  The chief executive customarily produces a report that focuses on the accomplishments of the organization during the period in between board meetings. This can include the status of new programs, updates on fundraising efforts, books published by the organization, or the announcement of new senior staff members.

- **Outsiders' Reports**

  Often, the board engages outside consultants or experts to facilitate or advise with projects such as the annual financial audit, strategic planning, a capital campaign, or a board self-assessment. The consultant may submit a written report detailing his or her findings or provide a status report of an ongoing project.

In addition to the written materials, the use of e-mail and a password-protected intranet can serve as an effective way to communicate information (including dashboards) to the board. Accessible through the organization's Web site, an intranet allows board members and the chief executive to post new information in a timely manner that may be quickly downloaded. It also offers opportunities for written discussions between members and for board members to share information with the rest of the board without having to wait until the next board meeting.

ASSESSING THE BOARD'S READINESS

Before plunging into the world of dashboards, board and staff leaders may need to step back and assess whether they are ready to commit to this task. Here's a quick reality check:

- Is the board satisfied with the information it currently receives?

- Does the board feel it needs more meaningful measures of performance or mission effectiveness?

- Does the board know what these measures should be?

- Do board members already know what it is that should be measured in a dashboard?

- What kinds of data are already being gathered and compiled to address the board's needs?

- How difficult would it be to provide the data to fuel the desired dashboard measures?

All the fuel gauges and warning lights in the world can't possibly tell a driver if he or she is on the wrong road. So, there needs to be a methodical process of determining what a governing board really must know in order to gauge whether it is achieving its mission goals and strategic objectives.

Additionally, there needs to be careful consideration of the effort and cost involved in gathering the requisite information. A cost-benefit mindset should be adopted that, at least as a starting assumption, requires any new data collection effort to be justified on the basis of

- how essential it is

- how costly it is to collect

- how accurate and timely it needs to be and is likely to be

What if, for example, it is determined that a dedicated annual survey is required to gauge the impact of a key program and no other means of assessing the program's impact is available? Further consideration should be given to minimizing the cost and effort of mounting such a survey by reducing or eliminating other less important data collection efforts and/or accomplishing multiple purposes through the same survey.

Boards should not succumb to the temptation of "incrementalism" — merely adding yet another layer of information to an already unwieldy array of reports for the board to absorb. After all, the whole point of dashboarding is to more efficiently get to the core issues and derive meaning from existing data — not to add to the board's burden of interpretation or to the staff's burden of data collection, processing, and presentation.

CREATING TRUST BETWEEN BOARD AND STAFF

By delegating the task of dashboard production to staff, the board must assume a level of confidence in the work of the staff and feel secure in the chief executive's ability to present trustworthy data on finances and programs. This means that staff is comfortable presenting not just the good news, but also the bad news. And particularly for organizations that have experienced a recent change in leadership or have had to dismiss a chief executive, it may take some time for the board to develop confidence in the new executive's ability. For these boards, it may not be an ideal time to embark on developing a dashboard reporting system.

On the other hand, a board that was dissatisfied with the data it received from an outgoing chief executive may find that a transition in leadership offers a good opportunity to rethink the data coming to the board. The board can set expectations early on, before a routine sets in, and avoid misinterpretation of what works, what is necessary, and what satisfies the board in its governance role.

2.
Defining Dashboard Metrics

Learning new information is a multistep process, beginning with awareness. Only after the appropriate players realize the essence and true value of dashboarding, as discussed in Chapter 1, can they do the prep work to really apply the knowledge gained from dashboard reports. If this preparation phase — building awareness and identifying appropriate elements to measure — is successful, the development of the dashboard itself will flow more easily. If the process becomes confused or cumbersome, the rest of the steps won't be easy.

MAINTAINING FOCUS AND SIMPLICITY

Flashy graphic displays in a dashboard format that highlight measurements of tactical or secondary consequence would only succeed in focusing the board's attention on the wrong things. The goal is focusing the board's attention on the *right* things.

The reality is that there is no single set of *right* things to measure for every organization and for every board; each board must choose what's best in regard to its current circumstances, and refrain from making it overly complicated. Where a board falls in its lifecycle may have a lot to do with what the board considers important to measure. A founding board that is establishing a new organization may have a set of concerns related to institutional establishment, formation, and initial survival. The board of an organization with a deeper history may want to assess its impact on a clientele or population group. Issues of outcome may be the primary focus for those organizations whose purpose is the promotion of particular, definable changes in the behavior, condition, or status of a population.

Organizations with more amorphous purposes of societal betterment may choose to focus on the quality of their services and the satisfaction levels of those they serve. And, because all boards have clear fiduciary obligations regardless of their institutional purpose or lifecycle stage, there may well be a common set of measures that assure any board of the financial solvency and ongoing viability of the enterprise.

DECIDING WHAT TO MEASURE

Having acknowledged the challenge of defining appropriate dashboard metrics and the varied perspectives that can be brought to bear, there are still ways of proceeding that can help get a board started on this important step. The following suggests six approaches to defining dashboard metrics:

1. Outcomes

2. Mission as spine

3. Strategic initiatives

4. Drivers of success

5. Risk factors

6. Service/resource matrix

These approaches are neither exhaustive nor mutually exclusive. Each offers a way to systematically identify performance indicators that are high-level in terms of their significance for institutional (or program) success, informative as to key aspects of organizational performance, and sensitive to critical changes, especially negative changes. Staff leadership, in collaboration with the board, should feel free to choose among these approaches and, if considered appropriate to their particular organizational experience and needs, combine features of these different approaches in moving toward a manageable set of meaningful dashboard metrics.

OUTCOMES

Any organization with a mission that aims to produce a societal benefit, especially one that seeks through specific programs to produce some sort of change in a defined population, needs to address the question of how it should measure its success by first defining the beneficial changes it seeks to achieve (outcomes). As the United Way of America Web site characterizes it: "Outcomes are not how many worms the bird feeds its young, but how well the fledgling flies."[4]

Outcome measurement is the gold standard when it comes to defining dashboard metrics because it comes closest to measuring a program or institution's ultimate effectiveness in pursuit of its mission. In *Measuring Program Outcomes: A Practical Approach*, United Way of America defines outcome measurement as the "regular systematic tracking of the extent to which program participants experience the benefits or changes intended."

There are, of course, other program components that can be measured in the course of assessing an organization's overall efficiency, productivity, fiscal responsibility, and operational effectiveness:

- **Inputs**

   Inputs are defined by the resources that are dedicated to or consumed by the program, such as money, staff and staff time, volunteers and volunteer time, facilities, and equipment and supplies.

- **Activities**

   Activities describe what the program does with inputs to fulfill its mission. For instance: feed and shelter homeless families; provide job training; educate the public about signs of child abuse; counsel pregnant women; or create mentoring relationships for youth.

---

4. See *Measuring Program Outcomes: A Practical Approach*. Alexandria, VA: United Way of America, 1996.

- **Outputs**

   Outputs classify the direct products of program activities. For example: number of classes taught; number of counseling sessions conducted; number of educational materials distributed; hours of service delivered; or number of participants served.

But none of the above can be classified as outcomes — the defined benefits or changes for participants as the direct result of program activities. Some examples of outcomes are new knowledge, increased skills, changed attitudes or values, improved condition, or altered status.

Increasingly, regulatory, accrediting, and funding agencies, as well as private foundations and individual donors, are insisting that governing boards of charitable and social service agencies and even institutions with more broadly defined health, educational, and cultural missions demonstrate that they have a disciplined process of outcome definition and measurement in place. Committing to outcome measurement requires a clear and robust theory of change to articulate the desired changes that result from the organization's activities in relation to its audiences, clientele, or participants (see page 52 for more information on the theory of change).

Defining outcomes can be difficult, especially in the case of organizations with broad missions. Even if a relatively amorphous outcome within a population of soup kitchen visitors like "saved lives through nourishment" were measurable, say, via follow-up tracking of these visitors over time, it may be difficult to gauge precisely the extent to which the soup kitchen itself created that outcome. It is well worth making the effort, though, as doing so helps to clarify the organization's purposes and sharpen its methods.

MISSION AS SPINE

Another approach to defining dashboard metrics begins with the organization's mission. Think of the mission as the spine of the enterprise — the essential, underlying framework of values and purpose that gives it shape and resiliency. By recasting the mission as a set of phrases that speak to the organization's purpose(s), audience(s), or populations served, this set of phrases becomes the spine upon which relevant performance indicators can be hung. Even complex mission statements can be broken down and key mission themes identified.

Figure 4 on the next page is an example of the mission spine and selected performance indicators for a natural history museum. The mission statement happens to be a single sentence: "The Sample Museum of Natural History tells the story of our planet and its inhabitants to families and students of all ages through artifacts, specimens, and programs that reveal the process of scientific research and discovery, leading to an appreciation of how scientists answer current questions while raising new ones." When broken into its component phrases, it becomes possible to define performance indicators or metrics that speak to the institution's success at fulfilling its mission imperatives of purpose, audience, methods, and outcomes.

Even if their mission statements aren't as specific or concise as this one, most organizations should be able to address each of these four mission imperatives. If not found in the actual mission statement, the pertinent language typically exists in fundraising and marketing materials. And if the information is not there, then the effort of creating dashboard reports built upon a mission spine can itself be the catalyst for bringing clarity to the organization's mission.

Figure 4

Mission Statement			
Purpose	Audience	Methods	Outcomes
The Sample Museum of Natural History tells the story of our planet and its inhabitants...	to families and students of all ages...	through artifacts, specimens, and programs that reveal the process of scientific research and discovery...	leading to an appreciation of how scientists answer current questions while raising new ones.
Performance Indicators			
Number of exhibits and programs that use stories and engaging narratives. Diversity of human cultures and other living species featured in these stories.	Percentage of admissions, memberships, and other participants who are families and students, by age.	Involvement of scientists in presenting their research agenda/results. Use of collection of specimens and artifacts for educational purposes.	Visitor responses re: lessons learned about the scientific method of inquiry and before/after appreciation of scientific research.

STRATEGIC INITIATIVES

Strategy can seem far more complicated than it needs to be. In its book *Strategic Decision Making: Key Questions and Indicators for Trustees*, the Association of Governing Boards of Universities and Colleges (AGB) defines strategy for purposes of this discussion:

> Strategic issues are ... associated with effectiveness in ... the few areas which are critical to the success of the institution. The key ... for most organizations is to focus their most limited resources — the time of trustees and top administrators — on those issues which really make the difference between success and failure.[5]

---

5. Frances, Carol, et al. *Strategic Decision Making: Key Questions and Indicators for Trustees*. Washington, DC: Association of Governing Boards of Universities and Colleges, 1987.

When the board, in collaboration with the chief executive and staff, has compiled the set of strategic issues deemed most relevant to the organization, the question arises as to how to translate a concern about any one of these issues into a means of assessing the organization's effectiveness, performance, or status in relation to that issue.

This process of translating concern about a strategic issue into a dashboard indicator is illustrated in Figure 5. In this case, a college's board is concerned about how a declining applicant pool might affect the institution's ability to maintain its selectivity standards.

Figure 5

STRATEGIC ISSUE: INFLUENCING THE SELECTIVITY OF THE INSTITUTION

Questions	Key Indicators
What is the image of the institution?	• Self-selection among applicants
How popular is the institution among potential students?	• Popularity index (number of applicants per matriculating freshmen or transfers)
How strong is the drawing power of the institution on students who have applied?	• Admission drawing power index (matriculants as a percentage of admitted freshmen and transfers) • Surveys of students who decline admission
How successful is the institution in retaining students through graduation?	• Retention index (percentage of freshmen who graduate)
What would be the impact on the applicant pool of changing student selectivity?	• Projected number of qualified applicants based on SAT or ACT cutoff scores
What would be the impact on incoming student quality of more (or fewer) matriculants?	• Projected SATs or ACTs of students based on different enrollments
Will the image of the institution help or hinder the recruitment of desired students?	• Image studies among potential and random students
How effective are the institution's recruitment materials and plans in stimulating applications and matriculations?	• Communications audits of recruitment materials and plans

Adapted from *Strategic Decision Making: Key Questions and Indicators for Trustees* by Carol Frances et al. Washington, DC: Association of Governing Boards of Universities and Colleges, 1987

This example presents several ways the board can understand the interplay between a decreasing applicant pool and the pressure to decrease selectivity. They may want to use a combination of different types of indicators — some quantitative (popularity and admission drawing power indices) and some qualitative (surveys and image studies). The precise number and combination of indicators needed to ensure effective monitoring of any particular issue will vary with each board's level of concern and the institution's capacity to produce or access the requisite information.

Ultimately, strategy drives measurement. If a strategic plan already exists, the major strategic themes, directions, or initiatives identified in the plan can and most likely should define the dashboard metrics. For example, a museum defined a set of dashboard performance indicators based on the strategic initiatives in its strategic plan, as shown in Figure 6.

Figure 6

Strategic Initiative	Goal	Performance Indicator
Build support for the museum.	Increase attendance by 10% per year.	Year-to-year changes in attendance
	Build membership by 10% per year and move 20% of renewals to higher levels.	Year-to-year changes in total membership and individual categories
Cultivate more diverse audiences.	Build a more diverse staff and board.	Demographic characteristics and trends on board and staff composition
	Attract new audiences and encourage repeat visitation.	Survey visitors in target audiences to determine visitation.
Make the museum a forum for different perspectives.	Schedule exhibits and programs that present different views on timely topics.	Analyze visitor comments to determine whether their interests and viewpoints are reflected in exhibit / program.
	Encourage visitors to share their perspectives with other visitors and with museum staff.	Track visitor use of "Talk Back" opportunities and publish responses in newsletter.

In the *absence* of a strategic plan, identifying appropriate dashboard measures will be a challenging effort, and it should drive the creation of a strategic plan as a priority for the organization.

DRIVERS OF SUCCESS

An organization may already have identified a set of outcomes, goals, or intermediary activities deemed essential for fulfilling its mission. How best to measure and monitor these drivers of success (sometimes called key performance indicators or critical success factors) then becomes the organizing principle of the dashboard design process.

The scorecard type of dashboard discussed earlier (Figure 2 on page 5) is an example of this approach as used by a hospital. A sample internship organization took a similar approach by deciding that its effectiveness was largely determined by maximizing the number of placement matches achieved and the number of weeks worked by each intern (or "Associate") and minimizing the number of work experiences cut short for various reasons ("Early Ends"). They designed a dashboard report featuring these measures (see Figure 7 on the next page).

RISK FACTORS

The board and senior staff may wish to adopt a more defensive posture and identify those worst-case situations that constitute grave threats to institutional survival or, at least, risk factors affecting organizational success. Indicators of campus security at a college, for example, might call for close monitoring not merely because of the liability implications but because of the inordinate damage that even a single unforeseen incident might cause to the institution's image and appeal to prospective students and their parents.

SERVICE/RESOURCE MATRIX

Another more generic approach to dashboard design is depicted in Figure 8 on page 19. It uses four broad categories related to the institution's services and resources viewed from both an internal and external perspective: service responsiveness, service quality, resource acquisition, and resource management. The particular performance measures focused on in each category would be dictated by mission considerations.

Service Responsiveness

In responding to the needs of the publics served, is the organization providing an appropriate mix of services? Is it meeting their needs? Service responsiveness might be gauged by client satisfaction scores, student retention rates, or trends in numbers of clients served. A dashboard report that highlights such indicators might not directly measure the services needed in a population, but could help the board understand the degree to which existing services are responding to existing needs. For example, a museum's mission that calls for enhancing appreciation of the cultural traditions of a particular ethnic community might require continuous tracking of pre- and post-visit perceptions of museum visitors.

Service Quality

Are the services being provided at an acceptable level of quality — acceptable to both the public and to the organization itself? Service quality indicators might

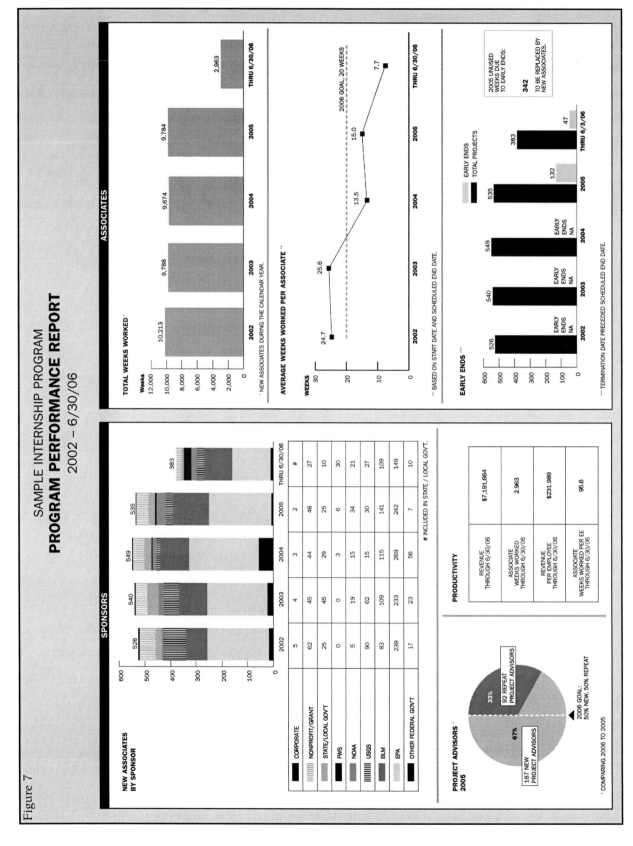

Figure 7

SAMPLE INTERNSHIP PROGRAM
PROGRAM PERFORMANCE REPORT
2002 – 6/30/06

SPONSORS

NEW ASSOCIATES BY SPONSOR

	2002	2003	2004	2005	THRU 6/30/06
	526	540	549	535	383
	#	#	#	#	#
CORPORATE	5	4	3	2	27
NONPROFIT/GRANT	62	45	44	48	10
STATE/LOCAL GOVT	25	45	29	25	30
FWS	0	0	3	6	21
NOAA	5	19	15	34	27
USGS	90	62	15	30	109
BLM	83	109	115	141	149
EPA	239	233	269	242	10
OTHER FEDERAL GOVT	17	23	56	7	

INCLUDED IN STATE / LOCAL GOVT.

ASSOCIATES

TOTAL WEEKS WORKED [*]

	2002	2003	2004	2005	THRU 6/30/06
Weeks	10,213	9,788	9,674	9,784	2,963

[*] NEW ASSOCIATES DURING THE CALENDAR YEAR.

AVERAGE WEEKS WORKED PER ASSOCIATE [**]

	2002	2003	2004	2005	THRU 6/30/06
WEEKS	24.7	25.6	13.5	15.0	7.7

2006 GOAL, 20 WEEKS

[**] BASED ON START DATE AND SCHEDULED END DATE.

EARLY ENDS [***]

EARLY ENDS
TOTAL PROJECTS

	2002	2003	2004	2005	THRU 6/3/06
TOTAL PROJECTS	526	540	549	535	383
EARLY ENDS	NA	NA	NA	132	47

[***] TERMINATION DATE PRECEDED SCHEDULED END DATE.

2005 UNUSED WEEKS DUE TO EARLY ENDS:

342

TO BE REPLACED BY NEW ASSOCIATES.

PRODUCTIVITY

REVENUE THROUGH 6/30/06	$7,191,664
ASSOCIATE WEEKS WORKED THROUGH 6/30/06	2,963
REVENUE PER EMPLOYEE THROUGH 6/30/06	$231,989
ASSOCIATE WEEKS WORKED PER EE THROUGH 6/30/06	95.6

PROJECT ADVISORS [*]
2005

33% / 92 REPEAT PROJECT ADVISORS
67% / 187 NEW PROJECT ADVISORS

2006 GOAL: 50% NEW, 50% REPEAT

[*] COMPARING 2006 TO 2005

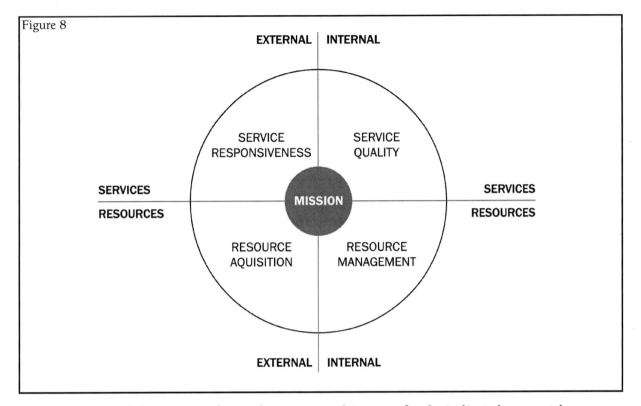

Figure 8

EXTERNAL | INTERNAL

SERVICE RESPONSIVENESS

SERVICE QUALITY

SERVICES
RESOURCES

MISSION

SERVICES
RESOURCES

RESOURCE AQUISITION

RESOURCE MANAGEMENT

EXTERNAL | INTERNAL

include measures of repeat business, complaints, or referrals. And/or indicators might explicitly gauge mission accomplishment or outcomes. For example, a nonprofit consulting business that stresses the highest standards in service delivery may monitor the quality of its services by sending out client surveys on a regular basis.

Resource Acquisition

How effectively is the organization acquiring the necessary resources? This may cover financial resources (e.g., donations, endowment value) as well as human resources (e.g., filling of key staff vacancies). For instance, a summer camp's mission to reach out to the underprivileged may require the organization to monitor fundraising for scholarships and other forms of support for disadvantaged children.

Resource Management

Is the organization managing its resources with proper stewardship? Is it efficient in its use of financial resources and fair in its dealings with constituents? These could include a whole range of financial indicators that speak to operational efficiency, budget adherence, and so forth. In the human resources realm, measures such as staff turnover could be monitored. For example, a hospital's mission that highlights the values of human dignity as well as fiscal integrity might call for monitoring of its debt collection procedures to ensure they are both humane and effective, for example, by setting reasonable collection periods and using a sliding payment scale.

The service/resource matrix, while more relevant to direct service providers, can be adapted to any nonprofit setting. *Services* would need to be defined in terms that fit the particular purposes of the organization. A charity with no easily identified clientele, for example, might interpret its services to be the attainment of research dollar goals.

It's All in the Interpretation

Once defined, dashboard metrics have only just begun to serve their purpose. To be useful they need to contain reliable data, be produced on a timely basis, and most importantly, be interpreted to inform meaningful decision making. A large piece of the puzzle is appropriate interpretation. As a consequence of how dashboards are understood, plans may need to be changed, investments increased, programs cut, staffing adjusted, or further research undertaken to better realize the meaning behind the numbers.

3.
Designing Dashboard Reports

Delivering information with intentional design contributes to meaningful interpretation. Once the board and staff have defined what it is the dashboard should measure, it is time to choose a format for the report. By using a combination of graphic charts, numbers, and descriptive text, the report takes shape and conveys a story. This chapter explains the theory behind dashboard design, offers specific tips for creating the reports, and describes ways in which a dashboard can reveal and add meaning to particular aspects of an organization's operations.

PRINCIPLES OF DESIGN

PRIORITY STRUCTURING: FIRST THINGS FIRST!

A board's time is its most scarce, and, in many ways, its most valuable resource. The board should be able to quickly locate the information it needs to know and at the level of detail it finds most relevant and comfortable.

The dashboard report helps the board and staff focus and prioritize. This type of presentation can be augmented with greater detail when the indicators reveal a potential problem or an issue to which the board should pay closer attention. For example, an unbudgeted loss shown on a dashboard report might require an additional page of detail on the expenses or services producing that loss.

Even though a dashboard report presents overall results, it may be necessary to break down some of the components. The key, of course, is not to go so far as to bury the board in excessive detail. Major service categories or business units, client populations, or geographical areas are the types of categories into which operating results might be broken down. Board members should be able to relate the changes and variances in these particular categories to the expected values. Displaying them with respect to each other and with respect to their budgeted and historical performance can help board members get a sense of how each category affects the overall results.

A social service agency, for example, created a financial dashboard (Figure 9 on the next page) that not only portrays actual versus budgeted year-to-date revenues, but breaks down the resulting total variance from budget by business units to better indicate which ones contributed positively or negatively to the total variance.

What the full board receives on a routine basis should be selective in the sense that it is the tip of an information iceberg that extends down to include board committees and task forces. While the full board may wish to see these data on a selective basis, greater levels of detail might be available on a routine basis to these committees and the staff supporting them. Coordinating committee and full board meeting agendas for the year makes it possible for certain topics to work their way up an agenda ladder to the full board at specific points during the year.

Figure 9

SAMPLE SOCIAL SERVICE AGENCY
MONTHLY STATUS REPORT
YTD January 31, 2007

REVENUE

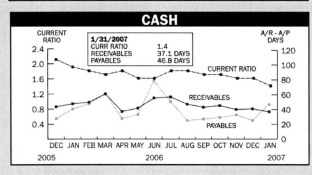

FY 2006 ← → FY 2007

- ADMIN
- RESOURCE DEVELOP
- CONTINGENT LABOR
- COMMERCIAL
- DIRECT SERVICES

$3,500,000 / 3,000,000 / 2,500,000 / 2,000,000 / 1,500,000 / 1,000,000 / 500,000 / 0

61%   56%   56%   50%

2006 ACT   2007 BUDG   YTD BUDG   YTD ACT

CASH

CURRENT RATIO

1/31/2007	
CURR RATIO	1.4
RECEIVABLES	37.1 DAYS
PAYABLES	46.8 DAYS

A/R - A/P DAYS

2.4 / 2.0 / 1.6 / 1.2 / 0.8 / 0.4

CURRENT RATIO
RECEIVABLES
PAYABLES

120 / 100 / 80 / 60 / 40 / 20 / 0

DEC JAN FEB MAR APR MAY JUN JUL AUG SEP OCT NOV DEC JAN
2005 — 2006 — 2007

CLIENT CENSUS

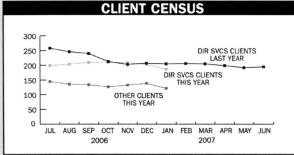

300 / 250 / 200 / 150 / 100 / 50 / 0

DIR SVCS CLIENTS LAST YEAR
DIR SVCS CLIENTS THIS YEAR
OTHER CLIENTS THIS YEAR

JUL AUG SEP OCT NOV DEC JAN FEB MAR APR MAY JUN
2006 — 2007

VARIANCE FROM BUDGET

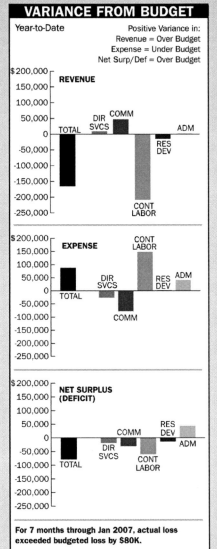

Year-to-Date

Positive Variance in:
Revenue = Over Budget
Expense = Under Budget
Net Surp/Def = Over Budget

REVENUE

$200,000 / 150,000 / 100,000 / 50,000 / 0 / -50,000 / -100,000 / -150,000 / -200,000 / -250,000

TOTAL, DIR SVCS, COMM, CONT LABOR, RES DEV, ADM

EXPENSE

$200,000 / 150,000 / 100,000 / 50,000 / 0 / -50,000 / -100,000 / -150,000 / -200,000 / -250,000

TOTAL, DIR SVCS, COMM, CONT LABOR, RES DEV, ADM

NET SURPLUS (DEFICIT)

$200,000 / 150,000 / 100,000 / 50,000 / 0 / -50,000 / -100,000 / -150,000 / -200,000 / -250,000

TOTAL, DIR SVCS, COMM, CONT LABOR, RES DEV, ADM

For 7 months through Jan 2007, actual loss exceeded budgeted loss by $80K.

NOTES

- Direct Services revenues on budget.
- Production revenues $161K under budget.
  ABC Co. +47K
  XYZ Co. -208K
- ABC: 16% over budget
  Proj: 53% over
- XYZ: 17% under budget
  Proj: 30% under

YTD 1/31/2007

		DIRECT SVCS	COMM	CONT LABOR	RES DEV	ADMIN O/H	TOTAL YTD ACTUAL	YTD BUDGET	VARIANCE
REVENUE		525,569	330,095	887,490	22,689	2,258	1,768,101	1,933,505	(165,404)
DIRECT EXPENSES	DIR COST	0	232,448	424,975	0	0	657,423	746,892	89,469
	STAFF EXP	396,790	114,565	76,792	13,158	273,112	874,417	813,350	(61,067)
	DIR OP'S	71,026	82,358	0	15,945	0	169,329	218,017	48,688
ADMIN ALLOC		91,188	124,000	124,000	18,237	(357,425)	- -	- -	- -
OVERHEAD		- -	- -	- -	- -	211,112	211,112	218,813	7,701
NET SURPL (DEF)		(33,435)	(223,276)	261,723	(24,651)	(124,541)	(144,180)	(63,567)	(80,613)

COMPARATIVE CONTEXT: COMPARED TO WHAT?

To derive meaning from raw data, or, in other words, to transform data into information, it is often useful to ask the question: Compared to what? Whenever possible, data should be presented in a manner that provides a comparative context. Even if experienced board members have a good sense of what the numbers mean, newer members will lack such a frame of reference and will need a basis for comparison. Comparisons can be made with historical data (e.g., same period last year), norms (e.g., strategic goals, budgets, forecasts, industry ratios), and benchmarks based on the performance of peer organizations (what are the other guys doing?). Data can also be displayed in the context of historical trends because they might reveal an emerging problem.

The dashboard referred to in Figure 9 combines comparisons of revenues with previous year-to-date numbers, variances from the budget, and trends in client population and in service volumes over time. These displays, shown together on a single page, give a multifaceted view of the organization's performance that raw data without a proper context cannot do. The Sample University expense dashboard (Figure 10.3 on page 26) uses comparative, contextual elements in two ways — by providing five-year trend data and peer group data.

Often, the very exercise of setting comparative or normative standards requires the board to think through what it considers to be an appropriate level of good or bad performance. In doing this, the board should look for guidance from its mission, values, and strategic concerns. An organization with a value stressing stewardship of resources, for example, might call for heightened concern about managing cash flow. This concern might cause the board to focus on, among other things, the management of accounts receivable and, more specifically, on reducing the collection period. Selecting an indicator such as "accounts receivable days" would serve the board's needs. But specifying a norm or performance standard of 60 days as opposed to 90 would more explicitly reflect the board's concern and permit the board to more readily interpret whether reported performance is good or bad.

The use of "what-if" scenarios is another way to enhance data interpretation through comparative context — in this case, the context of alternative futures. Once a board feels it has a good grasp of current performance and historical trends, it will often want to gain a better understanding of the possible future outcomes of particular policies, or of the impact various combinations of factors or events might have in the future. The simplest projection would extrapolate a trend that appears during the year to the full year (e.g., what if revenue remains 5 percent below budget for the remainder of the year?).

"What-if" projections can reveal the sensitivity of the organization's financial viability to changes in a key variable. The staff can also develop more elaborate models for examining scenarios of concern to the board — reflecting possible changes in pricing, competitor behavior, or governmental regulations. While dashboards by definition are not typically the best format for presenting what-if scenarios of any complexity, they can occasionally be used to alert the board to a range of possible outcomes.

Figure 10.1

SAMPLE UNIVERSITY
REPORT STRUCTURE

OVERVIEW

**What has been our overall
financial performance?**

Revenue

Expense

Surplus (Deficit)

REVENUE

Is our revenue structure balanced?

Tuition / Fees

Endowment

Gifts

EXPENSE

**Are we deploying
our funds appropriately?**

Instruction

Academic Support

Plant & Maintenance

RESOURCE ACQUISITION

**How well are we acquiring
the resources we need?**

Tuition / Financial Aid

Endowment

Development

RESOURCE MANAGEMENT

**How well are we using and
managing our resources?**

Physical Plant

Faculty

Assets & Reserves

STUDENTS

**Are we attracting and keeping
the kinds of students we want?**

Enrollment

Student Profile

Attrition

Figure 10.2

INCOME

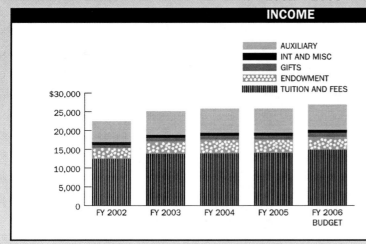

Total income increased 11.6% between 2001-2002 and 2004-2005.

Income from auxiliary services, while second only to tuition and fees as a source of income, is largely offset by auxiliary expense (see below).

EXPENSE

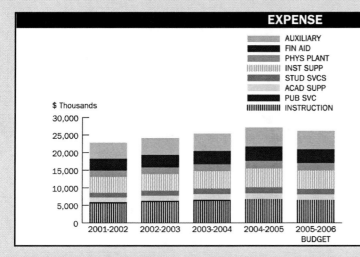

Significant components of expense and their average percent of total education and general expense (total expense less auxiliary) over the past four years are:

Instruction	**34 %**
Instit Support	**22 %**
Financial Aid	**20 %**

SURPLUS (DEFICIT)

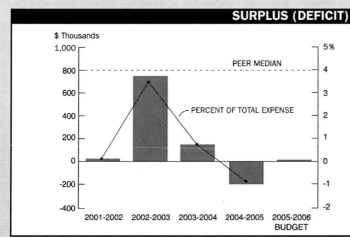

Sample University has operated generally on a break-even basis, earning a surplus of $753K in 2002-2003 – or 3% on total expenses.

Net surplus from auxiliary services contributed $300K on average per year.

Figure 10.3

SAMPLE UNIVERSITY
EXPENSE
FY 2002 – 2005

INSTRUCTION

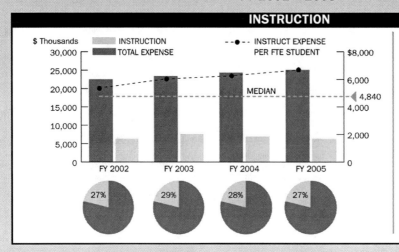

Instruction expense continues to run close to the 30% median level overall.

Per FTE student, Sample University at $6,752 is significantly higher than the median.

PEER GROUP MEDIAN	PEER GROUP PERCENTILES
30%	95TH: 38%
	50TH: 30%
	5TH: 15%

ACADEMIC SUPPORT

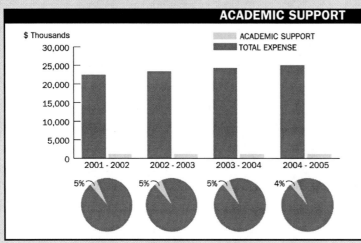

Academic support continues to run at the 5% median level.

PEER GROUP MEDIAN	PEER GROUP PERCENTILES
5%	95TH: 13%
	50TH: 5%
	5TH: 2%

PLANT / MAINTENANCE

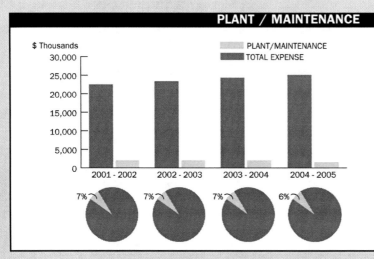

Plant & Maintenance has been running at a stable 7–6% – about two-thirds the median percentage.

PEER GROUP MEDIAN	PEER GROUP PERCENTILES
9%	95TH: 18%
	50TH: 9%
	5TH: 4%

Brief Explanations: What's the Point?

Limited amounts of accompanying text may help expand on the report's graphic or numeric indicators. Brief narrative summaries, for example, might describe the highlights of the previous time period. If the summaries are well written, they can tie together the links between current and past trends in ways that make it easier for the board to understand. Figure 3 (see page 7) is an example of a dashboard that includes comments describing how operating results are related to each other.

These narrative summaries would not replace the chief executive's regular report to the board, but can help him or her communicate the same information much more efficiently and thus leave more time for explanations, questions, and discussion.

Narrative Journeys: What's the Story?

The items presented in a dashboard report can be linked in a manner that tells a story to board members. For example, data might indicate how unexpected financial results, such as revenues below budget, are related to changes in volumes of services and/or changes in fees paid for those services.

A number of techniques can be employed to help tell the story. Along with the narrative comments box (discussed above), headlines can also be useful. These phrases lead the viewer's eyes from one display to another, highlighting their interrelationships.

The advantage of presenting information in a story format is that it helps interpret the information. The downside is that it can bias the reader and discourage board members from developing their own insights. The tension between these two impulses — to actively guide the board in interpreting information or to empower the board to understand the information on its own terms — will always exist. It can be difficult to find a balance between the two that satisfies all boards or be appropriate to all situations.

The extent to which a board welcomes, or even tolerates, staff guidance will be conditioned by the culture of the board and by its level of confidence in the staff's ability to provide accurate, timely, and dependable information. A financial or public relations crisis, for example, might call for telling a straightforward story, whereas board members may want to develop their own interpretations of trends affecting long-range planning.

A dashboard report can lay the foundation for a more integrated or holistic picture and a productive, interactive discussion between board and staff. As such, the dashboard is only intended as a launching point to understanding the full story.

Figures 10.2 and 10.3 (see pages 25 and 26) attempt to strike a balance between empowerment and guidance of board members by including narrative comments that clarify the graphic material. These comments, while drawing attention to the most important points or trends, nevertheless stop short of explaining their strategic significance.

When the underlying story is not evident from an array of facts — presented in numerical and graphic displays, plus narrative points — a more explicit, storyline linkage between key indicators may be called for. Figure 11 reconstructs a story from some of the more significant indicators that appear in the preceding pages. While still lacking editorial comment, it is a more direct attempt at revealing the compelling story hidden within the data.

Only so much of a story can be captured in brief bullet points, however. Don't underestimate the value of anecdotes to round out the picture. Client stories can be used to

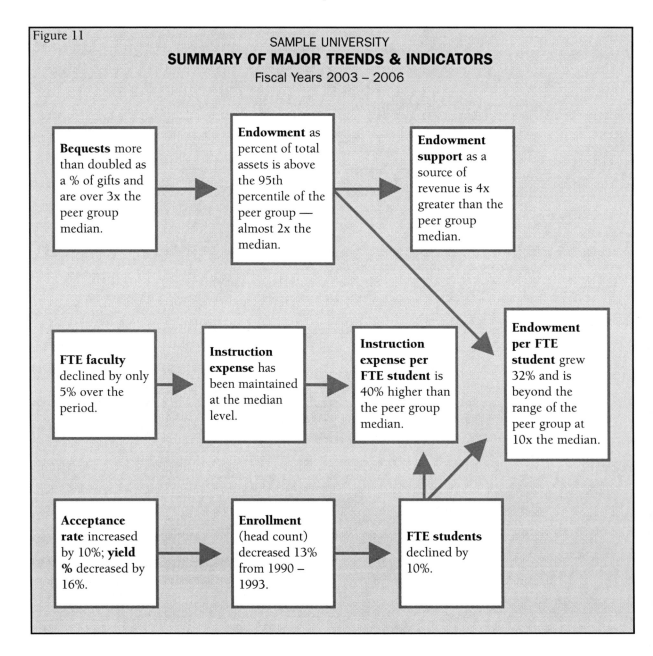

Figure 11

SAMPLE UNIVERSITY
SUMMARY OF MAJOR TRENDS & INDICATORS
Fiscal Years 2003 – 2006

Bequests more than doubled as a % of gifts and are over 3x the peer group median.

Endowment as percent of total assets is above the 95th percentile of the peer group — almost 2x the median.

Endowment support as a source of revenue is 4x greater than the peer group median.

FTE faculty declined by only 5% over the period.

Instruction expense has been maintained at the median level.

Instruction expense per FTE student is 40% higher than the peer group median.

Endowment per FTE student grew 32% and is beyond the range of the peer group at 10x the median.

Acceptance rate increased by 10%; **yield %** decreased by 16%.

Enrollment (head count) decreased 13% from 1990 – 1993.

FTE students declined by 10%.

illustrate mission impact, putting a human face on the numbers. Stories bring the dashboard to life and, therefore, are an important part of the board information system.

GRAPHIC ENHANCEMENT: WHAT'S THE BIG PICTURE?

This is, again, where it becomes important to keep in mind the different levels of detail that staff routinely receive versus what the board needs to see. Many of the examples cited in this book demonstrate that using certain basic graphic display techniques can make otherwise obscure, statistical reports not only comprehensible but also dramatic and powerful in portraying the big picture to the board. Through the use of line charts, bar graphs, pie charts, and data maps in place of dense tables of numbers or text, large amounts of information can be conveyed more efficiently and in ways that add meaning by revealing important patterns and causal relationships.

The Sample University reports in Figures 10.1, 10.2, and 10.3 for example, were derived from the institution's annual fact book — a 50-page compendium of numerical data densely arrayed in page after page of columns and rows. The facts were there for the board to see, but it was the rare board member who ever ventured into this data swamp. Through graphically enhanced dashboard formatting of key elements taken from that book, the board now has a fighting chance of interpreting the data.

These report pages appeal to the right *and* left brain through a combination of graphic, numeric, and narrative elements. The goal in combining numbers, words, and graphics is not to guarantee that each board member receives exactly the same message in the same way, but rather to empower each board member to derive his or her own meaning from the data. By posing questions and sharing perspectives with one another, the board emerges with a collective understanding that is richer and more complete than that of any individual.

The graphic overview structure diagram in Figure 10.1 that introduces the reports in Figures 10.2 and 10.3 serves as a kind of road map, showing the interrelationships among the various reports. It also provides a conceptual framework that can orient the user over time. For example, although the various reports that make up this particular set can be viewed as a single package produced annually, they need not be presented to the board all at once. Certain reports can be reviewed by different board committees at different points during the year. In fact, the board as a whole might only need to see the broadest trend data displayed graphically, while board committees would receive a more granular depiction and staff an even greater level of detail.

In his book *The Visual Display of Quantitative Information*, Edward Tufte provides a number of useful ideas for presenting information graphically. Some of his principles of good graphic design are the following:

- *Avoid misleading distortions.* For example, the use of year-to-date numbers rather than month-to-month changes may help the board avoid focusing too much attention on random variations that have little significance. Similarly, avoid scales that exaggerate the importance of certain trends (e.g., percentage changes in small numbers).

- *Focus attention on the substance rather than the method of presentation.* Ironically, the very ease with which complex graphic displays can be created has contributed to unnecessary embellishment that may dazzle the eye but distract from the data's message.

- *Use more than one set of graphic displays on a page.* Combining multiple graphic messages on a single page and avoiding the need to flip through several pages to get the same information encourages the eye to compare and, in so doing, spot patterns and relationships among them.

Tufte refers to a particularly effective way to harness the visual power of many small graphic displays all using the same scales on a single page. He calls them "small multiples." Figure 12 is a dense tabular report that had been presented to a senior-care holding company showing 12 months of current ratios for each of 12 elderly housing and nursing home facilities. The board found it very difficult to decipher. When these same data were converted into small multiples (Figure 13 to the right), they quickly revealed which facilities had been consistently experiencing negative ratios (in black) from those with positive ratios (in grey).[6]

Figure 12

SAMPLE SENIOR CARE NETWORK
CURRENT RATIOS (CURRENT ASSETS/CURRENT LIABILITIES)
12 MONTHS ENDING 1/31/2007

FACILITY	FEB '06	MAR '06	APR '06	MAY '06	JUN '06	JUL '06	AUG '06	SEP '06	OCT '06	NOV '06	DEC '06	JAN '07
ANDERSON	1.15	1.08	1.10	1.09	1.08	1.10	1.09	1.11	1.07	1.07	1.03	1.00
BENNINGTON	1.14	1.13	1.11	1.00	0.93	0.94	0.54	0.52	0.66	0.75	0.76	0.72
BRUNSWICK	1.05	1.01	1.66	1.67	1.67	1.31	1.38	1.41	1.25	1.29	1.28	1.15
CLYDESVILLE	1.84	1.10	0.99	1.00	1.05	1.14	1.19	1.17	0.68	0.74	0.74	0.91
COLUMBUS	1.22	1.32	1.75	1.53	1.76	1.45	1.65	1.69	1.59	1.57	1.41	1.38
HAMILTON	0.76	0.87	1.00	1.03	1.41	1.48	0.89	1.43	1.24	1.41	1.46	1.34
JEFFERSON	0.54	0.47	0.72	0.75	1.05	0.96	1.83	1.17	1.46	1.43	1.38	1.09
LAKEVIEW	0.66	0.67	0.67	0.75	0.79	0.94	1.02	0.90	0.92	0.98	0.95	0.69
LAUREL	0.84	0.76	0.77	0.76	0.70	0.75	0.76	1.02	1.04	1.06	1.02	0.91
LIBERTY	1.02	1.02	0.79	1.00	1.45	1.38	1.57	1.87	1.77	1.90	1.85	1.88
RIVERWAY	0.86	0.68	0.67	0.63	0.71	0.45	0.54	0.67	0.66	0.66	0.65	0.80
WADSWORTH	1.65	1.71	1.78	1.78	1.77	1.77	1.75	1.77	1.79	1.81	1.72	1.59

CHOOSING DATA DISPLAY FORMATS — HELPFUL HINTS

The formats chosen for displaying data can either clarify or obscure their meaning. The following (beginning on page 32) are suggestions to help make the meaning of data as clear and transparent as possible.

---

6. *See* Tufte, Edward R. *The Visual Display of Quantitative Information.* Cheshire, CT: Graphics Press, 2001.

Figure 13

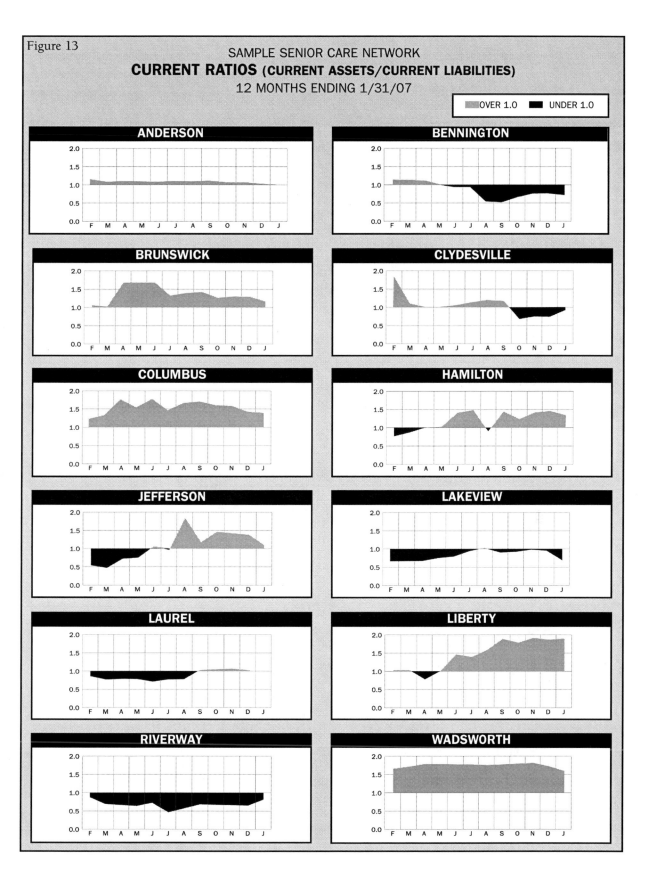

SAMPLE SENIOR CARE NETWORK
CURRENT RATIOS (**CURRENT ASSETS/CURRENT LIABILITIES**)
12 MONTHS ENDING 1/31/07

OVER 1.0   UNDER 1.0

LEFT-TO-RIGHT TIME SERIES

It can be disconcerting for viewers to have to work against a natural impulse in reading charts or data tables. Most people are accustomed to reading from left to right. The same rule should be adopted in the presentation of time series data. The earliest time period in the series should be placed to the left and the more recent periods to the right.

PIE CHARTS

Pie charts are great for immediately conveying the notion of percentage shares of a particular total quantity. When it comes to *comparing* pie charts, however, the human eye can have difficulty discerning small differences in the sizes of pie slices, especially when they occur at different angles in adjacent charts. To make the comparison clearer, each slice should be properly labeled with its particular value — either within or adjacent to the slice. The pie chart should also indicate the absolute value of the pie itself. However, this can be misleading when comparing two pie charts that differ in their total values but are depicted at the same size. Combining pie charts and column or bar charts, such as shown in Figure 10.3 on page 26, helps to convey both absolute value as well as percentage share differences.

STACKED COLUMNS

Stacked columns (vertical bars as shown in the New Associates by Sponsor section of Figure 7, on page 18) can be a useful alternative to multiple pie charts. The components of the column represent the relative shares of a total amount as well as the absolute value of that total. This can be particularly helpful when the stacked columns are arrayed in a time series. Including the numerical value for each of the stacked bar units makes it much easier to identify the value of each of the components, whereas relying solely on the vertical scale to the left of the bars to gauge the values can be difficult.

DATA TABLES

One way to provide the numerical support for any graphic chart without cluttering the chart itself with too many numbers is to create a data table below the chart. As the same chart in Figure 7 demonstrates, this format conveys both the graphic's visual appeal and the hard data all within the same visual space.

LINE CHARTS INSTEAD OF SIDE-BY-SIDE COLUMNS

A line chart, also referred to as a fever chart, connects points on a graph to show changes over time. Trying to convey the same value sets as side-by-side columns can become quite bewildering, as the columns (and the white spaces between sets of columns) are perceived as visually active. Essentially, a line chart connects the tops of related columns with separate lines, thereby eliminating the columns themselves. The eye is relieved of all this wasted visual activity and the trends and meaningful patterns become immediately apparent. The line chart titled "Monthly Paid Associates" in Figure 14 had previously consisted of a visually chaotic array of side-by-side columns representing different time periods.

Figure 14

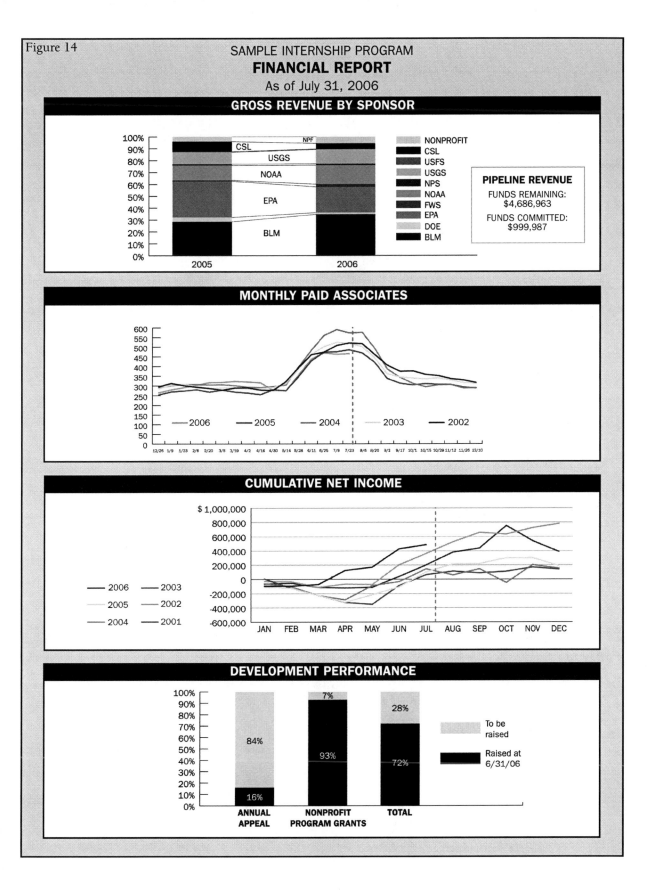

SAMPLE INTERNSHIP PROGRAM
FINANCIAL REPORT
As of July 31, 2006

GROSS REVENUE BY SPONSOR

PIPELINE REVENUE

FUNDS REMAINING:
$4,686,963

FUNDS COMMITTED:
$999,987

MONTHLY PAID ASSOCIATES

CUMULATIVE NET INCOME

DEVELOPMENT PERFORMANCE

These same data presented as a set of lines differentially colored by time period reveal both the underlying seasonal trends and the different levels of activity associated with each year.

OPTIONS FOR COMMUNICATING A SPECIFIC DASHBOARD FOCUS

Chapter 1 refers to an art museum dashboard report (Figure 3) that uses many of the features typically built into the dashboard format. There are other types of dashboards that emphasize one or more of these features (financial or program status) or are for-matted in ways that bring attention to particular aspects of the organization's operations (warning light reports or work flow diagrams). The following examples show how dashboards lend themselves to creative formatting.

FINANCIAL DASHBOARDS

Financial dashboards summarize financial information that the board would expect to see in traditional financial statements, but in a much more readily digestible form.

The financial dashboard referred to in Figure 9 on page 22 attempts to capture various aspects of the agency's financial status on a single page. Because this particular board meets monthly and wishes to maintain a fairly current view of financial performance, it values a dashboard that displays not only cumulative revenue and expense, and net surplus (deficit), but also includes monthly cash flow data. The revenue and expense performance is presented in a bar graph highlighting comparisons to the previous year's values. Numerical tables were also included for board members who prefer to view the data in a more precise format.

PROGRAM DASHBOARDS

Programs deliver a defined set of services or experiences to an audience, market, or defined population. They represent the real-world manifestations of organizational mission and, therefore, are of great interest to boards. This interest typically requires understanding the program content, the quality of program delivery, and the extent and nature of program impact on those being served.

Data about program performance can be difficult for board members to interpret without a basic understanding of program structure and content. Board members most likely will not have the same kind of detailed understanding of the program that staff members do. For staff members more intimately familiar with a program, it is easy to assume that board members understand the program's content and objectives, and to develop shorthand terms for talking about programs and use unfamiliar acronyms, ultimately confusing the uninitiated even further.

Program dashboards can speak to the board's needs by focusing on the following:

- **Program outcomes** in the sense described in Chapter 2 as the desired benefits or changes that participants experience as the result of program activities, and the systematic tracking of performance indicators that measure these benefits or changes.

- **Program components** and how they relate to each other. Focusing on individual components one at a time may keep board members from seeing the big picture. Board members need to see how clients flow from one service component to another and how services may be combined with others to achieve desired outcomes.

- **Resources utilized** describes the number and type of staff (or other costs) associated with a particular program. The report can also show which programs are resource intensive (e.g., low client-to-staff or revenue-to-staff ratio).

- **Client population** describes who the programs serve in terms of demographic or other characteristics.

Program dashboards can also benefit from the use of graphics. Flow diagrams, for example, can help the board understand the movement of clients among program components as they receive services. Figure 15 (on the next page) was designed to help a social service agency better understand its client flow. The diagram depicts both numbers of clients in various programs at a point in time and the flow into, out of, and between components during the previous time period. Here measures are displayed at the intake and evaluation, work, pre-placement, and placement phases of the client flow.

Most importantly, it helps the board see the components in relation to each other, rather than as isolated entities. The flow diagram provides a common framework within which board and staff can discuss the program and interpret various data (e.g., outcomes and attrition rates at various points).

WARNING LIGHT REPORTS

A great deal of routine data reporting can be eliminated by specifying the range of outcomes the board would consider acceptable and the point at which it would want to be alerted if performance began to deviate either positively or negatively.

The board can then receive a "warning light" report, shown in Figure 16 on page 37, providing assurance that each of a whole series of factors is being monitored. It is only when performance has exceeded some agreed-upon threshold that the "light" will flash on.

In Figure 2 (page 5) we saw how a summary dashboard uses a red downward pointing arrow icon to focus the board's attention on performance indicators that had strayed beyond a reasonable variance from a benchmark or goal value. This is a kind of warning light report. Figure 3 (page 7) also includes a variation of the warning light feature (not illustrated in this publication). When any of the windows in the report contains information revealing problems or raising concerns, the small numbered box in the upper left corner of each of the windows can be designed to flash red and then explained in the comment window. Windows containing

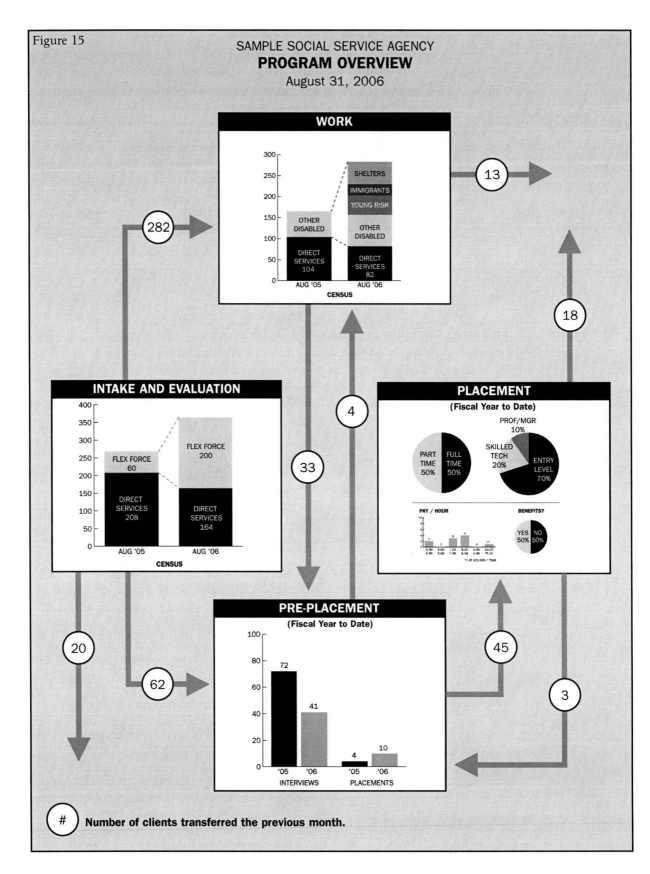

Figure 15

SAMPLE SOCIAL SERVICE AGENCY
PROGRAM OVERVIEW
August 31, 2006

WORK

SHELTERS
IMMIGRANTS
YOUNG RISK
OTHER DISABLED
DIRECT SERVICES 82

OTHER DISABLED
DIRECT SERVICES 104

AUG '05   AUG '06
CENSUS

13

18

282

INTAKE AND EVALUATION

FLEX FORCE 60

FLEX FORCE 200

DIRECT SERVICES 208

DIRECT SERVICES 164

AUG '05   AUG '06
CENSUS

4

33

PLACEMENT
(Fiscal Year to Date)

PROF/MGR 10%

PART TIME 50%   FULL TIME 50%

SKILLED TECH 20%   ENTRY LEVEL 70%

PAY / HOUR

BENEFITS?
YES 50%   NO 50%

*1 AT $20,000 / YEAR

20

62

PRE-PLACEMENT
(Fiscal Year to Date)

72

41

4   10

'05   '06   '05   '06
INTERVIEWS   PLACEMENTS

45

3

Number of clients transferred the previous month.

Figure 16

FINANCIAL RESOURCES WARNING LIGHT REPORT	
○ **OPERATING INCOME RATIO** **Operating Income ÷ E&G Expenses**	
◦○ **CONTRIBUTED INCOME RATIO** **Contributed Income ÷ E&G Expenses** **8%**	Has fallen below the warning light threshold of 10%. Down from 12% last year. Education and General (E & G) expense has remained relatively constant, but unrestricted private gifts and grants have declined from $6.8 million last year to $4.6 million this year.
○ **DEBT BURDEN** **Debt Service ÷ Total Expenditures**	
◦○ **DEBT COVERAGE** **Adj. Change in Net Assets ÷ Debt Service** **2.4 x**	Has fallen below the warning light threshold of 2.5 x. Last year's debt coverage was 2.75 x. There was a greater than expected decline in unrestricted net assets from $4.6 million last year to $1.4 million this year.
○ **LEVERAGE** **Unrestricted and Temporarily Restricted Net Assets ÷ Debt Outstanding**	

Figure 17

SAMPLE NONPROFIT AGENCY
STRATEGIC DASHBOARD
May 31, 2006

MEASURES OF STRATEGIC SUCCESS

CLIENT POPULATION GROWTH
Clients served to date tracking closely with targeted level. We expect to reach the 1,850 target by September 2006.

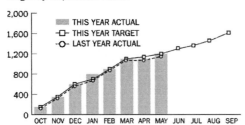

AGENCY REPUTATION
Have continued upward trend in responses from survey of funding agencies and constituencies. Approaching the high of last year. Greatest gains in name recognition.

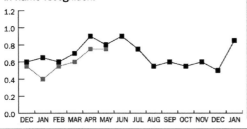

NEW GRANTS
Total value of new grants year-to-date close to budget, but mix has shifted toward state sources. Only two foundation grants rather than the four projected.

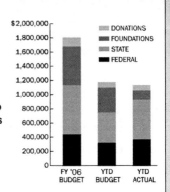

SERVICE OUTCOMES
Compared to last year, 10% fewer clients this year have experienced long term positive disposition of their cases. Short term positive dispositions have increased slightly. Negative outcomes have remained constant.

ENABLERS

NEW PROGRAM DEVELOPMENT
Three major new programs launched this year compared to only one last year.

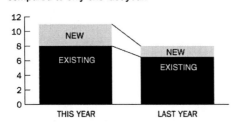

MARKETING / OUTREACH
New video and brochures now being distributed. Three additional mass mailings are scheduled for January 2007.

CAPACITY DEVELOPMENT
Upgrading of computer capabilities on schedule. New intake center to open in November 2006 will increase our client capacity by 20%.

DETERRENTS

WAITING TIME
With exception of March and April, have maintained waiting time at or below 40 minutes.

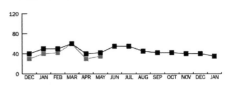

CLIENT SATISFACTION
Client survey shows a 17% improvement in favorable ratings over last year.

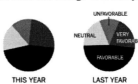

NEGATIVE INCIDENTS
No incidents in the last six months. 2005 lawsuit settled in March.

information of a positive or expected nature can be designed to flash green and commented upon only if deemed necessary.

Warning lights can be created to show when adherence to some aspect of mission (e.g., a certain percentage of single mothers housed in shelters, a percentage of books donated to inner city schools) has fallen below acceptable levels.

STRATEGIC DASHBOARDS

When operational performance data are linked to mission and strategic initiatives, they convey greater insights. For example, if the organization plans to grow significantly and has invested resources for growth, data might be displayed in a manner that distinguishes new levels of activity from traditional performance. For the organization that is introducing a new program or serving a different client population, additional detail on these new activities may be warranted.

An organization might even create a strategic dashboard by selecting indicators of overall strategic success and displaying them in a way that also maintains the board's focus on factors that contribute to that success (enablers), as well as those that work against it (deterrents). Figure 17 (to the left) presents one way these various strategic indicators might be organized on a single dashboard page.

4.

Starting a Dashboard Program

The process of developing a dashboard reporting system — especially if it is part of a broader examination of the board's information resources — can be every bit as important as the report formats it produces. But creating and maintaining this reporting system requires a structured process and dedicated attention by both board and staff.

Improving board information can serve as an excellent point of entry for meaningful introspection and dialogue within the board and with staff on a broad range of important subjects, from the board's working relationship with senior staff to the organization's mission and strategy. And, if done properly, the process of dashboard development can not only produce meaningful, high-level metrics, but can engender a strong sense of board ownership of those metrics.

BUILDING BOARD-STAFF COLLABORATION

Boards interested in embarking on a dashboard development program, or a broader examination of governance information, should initiate the process of the dashboard report's design and implementation. The governance committee (or another committee charged with overseeing internal board operations) may be tasked with guiding the development of a board-staff task force or working group that may include the board chair, the chief executive, a few board members, and one key staff person who will have the ongoing responsibility of accessing needed data and maintaining the system over time. The active involvement of the chief executive is an important signal to the staff that this work is of high priority and a truly collaborative effort. It is up to the staff to lead the process and communicate with the board on what it needs and wants.

DETERMINING THE BOARD'S NEEDS

As a first step, the task force will need to determine which elements make the most sense for inclusion in its dashboard development program.

1. Examine the information currently provided to the board. A good starting point for designing dashboard reports is to examine the information the board is presently receiving. This usually requires sitting down with the person who manages communications with the board (often the assistant to the chief executive) and reviewing a year's worth of information packets or meeting books. This review should provide a sense of the kind of information the board receives at each meeting and the items that are only sent out at certain times.

If there is an executive committee that meets more frequently than the full board and acts on its behalf, review the information sent to this group as well. Minutes of board and executive committee meetings might also be examined to see which items in the meeting books tend to provoke discussion and which items are relevant to actions taken by the board.

A review of other internal documents — from operating plans to reports sent to funding agencies — will reveal what information is already being collected. When information relevant to dashboard reporting is already being collected on a regular basis, it makes the whole exercise of creating dashboards more efficient and less daunting.

2. Interview key staff members. Supplement a review of the board's current information flows with interviews with the staff members who most closely interact with the board. This staff group would typically include the chief executive, chief financial officer, development director, and anyone else who works with the board or its key committees. The purpose of these interviews is to elicit the staff's perceptions of how the board uses information and of the types of information the board finds most valuable.

3. Ask board members what they need to know. The most straightforward way to identify the information and formats that will most help the board is to ask the board members themselves what information they need. This seems obvious, but more typically board members are given information that is produced as a byproduct of management information systems designed with different purposes in mind. In some cases, information is provided in response to a board member's one-time question only to become incorporated into a standard report that the board continues to receive long after it has ceased to be of any interest. In others, poor-performing boards might not even be clear as to their purpose or role, and may not act on guidance or requests from executive staff in the first place. These boards may only be interested in financial or operations measures rather than mission-focused information.

There are several ways to ask board members what they really need to know on an ongoing basis:

- **Interviews** of a cross-section of the board (including members who are heavily involved *and* those who are less active) can elicit many of the key variables that board members feel they need to monitor. The interviewer can help board members to distinguish between information that the board is accustomed to receiving and information that is actually used, and therefore important to continue receiving. The interviewer can also help board members to distinguish between information that the entire board needs, as opposed to items that are only appropriate for a specific committee.

- **Questionnaires** are another way to elicit the board's view of its information needs. These are especially useful with a large board or one whose members are geographically dispersed. The accompanying CD-ROM provides a sample board information survey that can easily be modified for any board. The questionnaire asks board members to rate how well the information they currently receive allows them to do their job and solicits suggestions for improving the information and its delivery system. Over time, the questionnaire can be periodically re-administered to assess where changes may be needed.

- **Focus groups** bring together board members for a focused discussion about board information needs. An advantage of a focus group is that comments made by one participant will often spark ideas and additional comments by others. A good facilitator can keep the discussion moving along, ask the right questions, and help record the insights that emerge. The discussion might focus on board roles, decisions, and organizational mission and goals as one set of topics. Another approach might be to have board members identify critical success factors for the organization (e.g., What must go right for us to do well? What must not go wrong?) and then to suggest indicators that reflect how well the organization is doing with respect to those factors. Focus groups can be used as the sole approach for gathering perceived information needs from the board, or in combination with interviews or questionnaires.

Whatever the technique(s) used, this process of information gathering should result in a relatively small set of variables that: a) are currently available, are used frequently, and tend to spark discussions; or b) are not currently available, but board members wish were available to use. For example, an organization may perceive service to indigent clients as an important part of its mission. However, as its board members think about mission, they might realize that they do not receive any information about the volume of services provided to indigent clients. This thought process can have great value, quite apart from how it shapes one or more dashboard reports.

4. Review "draft" formats with the board. Once a set of metrics has been identified for dashboard reporting, the next step is to find a suitable format for presenting it to the board. One of the best ways to develop an acceptable format is to create a first draft, show it to the board, and make the adjustments the board requests. Developing a dashboard is a very subjective process. What works for one person may not work for another. Showing a draft format to board members is likely to reveal displays that are unclear or misleading, important data items that are missing, and other problems that make the dashboard less useful than it could be. Several iterations might be necessary to get it right, but the final version should be one that the board is genuinely comfortable with and can adopt as its own. These iterations can involve the full board, if it has a small number of members and meets frequently, or can be done with a smaller group of members. The board-staff task force can be a very effective sounding board for this purpose.

WHAT ABOUT TIMING?

How often should dashboards be produced? Much depends on how frequently the needed data can be collected, when it would be most meaningful to interpret it, and when the board (or one of its committees) prefers to receive it.

For example, college enrollment data can only be collected when new students enroll. Typically, there is one major enrollment period per year. Collecting it more frequently is simply not possible, and reporting it more frequently than once a year would not be meaningful. On the other hand, cash flow and other financial data, especially in organizations concerned about their financial solvency, are typically collected monthly; the finance committee of the board, if not the board as whole, may want to receive a financial dashboard monthly. Similarly, risk factor data may require relatively frequent reporting so that the board can act in time to forestall negative consequences.

The board's meeting schedule over the course of the year can also determine which dashboard reports to receive and when. An annual board agenda plan that designates particular meetings for particular dashboards to be reviewed can assure the board that all of the key performance indicators or critical issues will be highlighted before the annual cycle of board meetings is completed.

MAINTAINING THE DASHBOARD REPORTING SYSTEM

No matter how well designed a dashboard reporting system is, its ongoing value to the board and the organization is only as good as the quality and timeliness of the data it reports and its perceived utility to board members and other users. The key to effective system maintenance is assigning responsibility for doing so to someone on the staff who has access to the relevant data and familiarity with the internal data systems, external databases, and application software (such as Excel® and PowerPoint®). Typically, this individual is already on staff and charged with providing administrative support to the board. If there is no such person already assigned these duties, someone should be designated.

This individual would be responsible for gathering all of the data required to populate the dashboards. Because dashboards often draw from multiple sources and databases inside (and sometimes outside) the organization, they require the intervention of someone charged with bringing the data together on a regular schedule to create the dashboard report(s). Ideally, this would be an automated process with the relevant databases linked to the reporting software. And, in many cases, this can be accomplished by integrating the dashboard report as a worksheet in an Excel® workbook (such as the dashboard generator on the CD-ROM) that also contains the database itself on another worksheet.

If a board-staff task force has already been established for purposes of assessing the board's information needs and assisting in the design of the dashboards, this group can continue to make improvements to the dashboards and pretest them on behalf of the board. But it is important to understand that the process of developing and maintaining the dashboard should be seen as an ongoing learning process that may never be finished — the initial dashboard report is *not* a finished product that only requires upkeep. Boards learn as they discover new and different things they want to know about. Over time, the reports may need to change focus or the task force may want to experiment with different levels of detail, identify alternative indicators, or discover new approaches to interpreting the data. The temptation, of course, is to keep adding more indicators until the dashboard looks like the cockpit of an airliner. Identifying new ways of looking at some dimension of the organization takes place over time, and the system is frequently under revision. For some boards, it could take a number of meetings to iron out a report's content and format. For others, the report may undergo regular revisions. Whatever a board's experience, it should be prepared to commit the time needed to work with staff on creating and maintaining the dashboard reporting system.

5.
Taking It On

The real test of whether dashboards have value is whether they create enough meaning for individual board members and the board as a whole to engender thought, insight, and, perhaps above all, good questions. The well-articulated, timely question that leads to further exploration of a critical issue, which in turn leads to answers that inform high-level decision making, is the ultimate payoff of dashboard reporting. Effective dashboards will strengthen the ability to engage each and every board member in a way that is meaningful for him or her, drawing forth the full range of wisdom, talent, and experience that resides on the board.

There are probably as many ways to work with dashboards to realize these benefits of critical thinking and board engagement as there are board members. The following are 10 common ways that have proven, in practice, to be valuable.

1. **Save time by reviewing highlights.**

   Dashboards are not meant to be a substitute for all of the information available to boards, but rather are designed as high-level overviews that combine an array of key indicators on a single page or on sets of pages. This allows them to fit naturally in board books as cover sheets that may appear on top of more detailed reports or online as a first level link in an increasingly detailed series of links, thereby permitting the user to drill down to greater levels of detail as needed. Just as with any logistical or navigational tool, dashboards can help the time-constrained board member employ his or her time more efficiently by using highlighted items in the dashboard as prompts to seek more detailed information.

2. **Track progress toward goals.**

   Dashboards can be used as tools for monitoring progress toward agreed-upon goals. The summary dashboard style (Figure 2) explicitly incorporates actual performance versus goals or benchmarks. Another example of this is a vision dashboard created in the context of strategic planning. Each strategic initiative from the plan will have a set of measures that tell the board whether the intended impact or effects of that initiative are being realized. A vision year is selected (maybe five or 10 years into the future) and the anticipated values for the various measures on the dashboard are set for that year. Depending on the time sensitivity of the measures in question, the board can request this dashboard at appropriate intervals (annually, semiannually, quarterly, etc.) and will be able to quickly gauge the progress (or lack thereof) that has been achieved in approaching the vision year value. Faced with inadequate progress, the board can ask some good questions as to underlying causes, which may result in: changing certain policies and practices that will better ensure attaining the vision year goal in question, modifying the goal itself, or some combination of both.

3. Understand system dynamics.

A dashboard like the one depicted in Figure 11 brings together a set of key ratios and other metrics in a way that conveys to the board the internal system dynamics of the organization. In this case, the relationships among faculty size, student enrollment, endowment growth, and various per-student metrics are explicitly highlighted. For those board members who have a limited understanding of how one factor can affect another in producing certain bottom line results, using a dashboard such as this can become a valuable board education tool.

4. Spot potential problems.

As was noted in Chapter 3, dashboards can be designed specifically as exception reports that alert the reader when certain performance metrics stray outside of acceptable ranges. These warning light reports (Figure 16) and the summary (scorecard) reports that use traffic light icons (Figure 2) are only as good as the metrics and ranges selected. When well constructed, boards can use these reports secure in the knowledge that certain critical factors are being closely monitored. If the board, for whatever reason, lacks confidence in an exception or icons-only style of reporting, dashboards that are more complete and yet structured around critical metrics (such as risk factors) can still serve to alert boards to potential problems in a timely manner.

5. Identify patterns and anomalies among similar entities.

One of the most common uses of dashboards is to array on a single page the performance results of multiple programs or business operating units. This enables the user to efficiently discern any patterns that all programs or units share and/or any anomalies that may call out for explanation.

The use of small multiples in Figure 13 is a good example of how a series of graphic displays that all employ the same scales quickly reveal which units have experienced positive or negative performance over the course of a year (in this case, in terms of ratios of current assets to current liabilities). Analyzing the same numbers in tabular form (Figure 12) would be considerably more difficult and time consuming. With the graphic dashboard, it is easier for a board member to spot the change in the operating unit labeled Clydesville and ask: "What happened last October to increase the current liabilities?"

6. Identify patterns and anomalies among diverse factors.

The same sort of rapid recognition of patterns and relationships can result from using dashboards that display on the same page a variety of factors or variables relating to a single entity. A museum board member viewing the dashboard in Figure 3 might look at the two monthly calendar charts and easily observe how cumulative income gets a boost when the monthly number of visitors increases. The board member may then be prompted to ask staff whether the drop-off in visitors in April and May of this year, especially in comparison with the average figures for the previous two years, is likely to have such a negative effect on cumulative income that the museum will miss its budget goal of approximately $1.9 million by the end of the fiscal year (four months from the time of the report). Will planned exhibitions generate sufficient visitors to compensate for this drop-off? If not, will there be sufficient income from other sources or cost savings to prevent a deficit for the year? Without having to look beyond this dashboard, the board member is equipped to ask a host of meaningful questions.

7. **Expand board member comfort zones.**

If the board member asking the above questions is a member of the finance committee, one might assume that his or her special interest in the museum's financial condition prompted these queries, the dashboard merely serving as a touchstone. But the board member might well have been a member of the curatorial committee who is typically far more interested in issues of an artwork's provenance or quality. When a dashboard's readily accessible metrics and graphic displays result in a board member expanding his or her comfort zone and becoming more fully engaged, then it's a gain for the entire board and organization.

8. **Bring all board members up to speed around a shared knowledge base.**

As the previous point illustrates, the more board members are conversant with multiple aspects of the organization's operations, the more effective the board can be as a governing team and, hence, the more valuable the board can be to the organization. Dashboards by themselves will not supply the shared knowledge base the board needs, but they can serve as a recurring reminder of the key factors at play and thereby equip all board members with a basic understanding of what makes the place tick. Incorporating the most recent set of dashboards in each new board member's orientation packet, coupled with an opportunity to review the dashboards under the guidance of a fellow board member serving as mentor, would be an excellent way to begin the process of sharing this knowledge base.

9. **Maintain a governance perspective.**

When a dashboard is designed with a governance perspective (gauging things like mission impact and outcomes, strategic effectiveness, and fiduciary oversight), it helps to encourage the board to perform its essential governance role rather than stray into some form of surrogate management role. In other words, dashboards can help to instill an organizationwide, policy-level perspective and reduce the tendency to micromanage from the boardroom. In a sense, the very process of defining dashboard metrics can be viewed as a collaboration exercise between board and senior staff, which clarifies the domains of governance and management.

10. Reinforce board oversight by linking to structure and process.

Finally, boards should be encouraged to use dashboards not only as stand-alone reports, but as key components in a more complete governance structure that also includes committee structure and meeting schedules and agendas. Dashboards, especially if they are built around mission imperatives or strategic themes, lend themselves to being cared for by a designated task force responsible for ensuring that dashboard data are accurate. Dashboards can be made the focus of particular board meetings and referred to at particular points on a meeting agenda. For example, a board's annual agenda plan may designate every Spring meeting to focus on quality of services. At that meeting, the quality committee could present the board with the "quality dashboard." In this way, all of a board's major oversight responsibilities can be ensured of receiving their moment in the spotlight . . . with the dashboard serving as the spotlight.

USING THE DASHBOARD GENERATOR

The accompanying CD-ROM contains a Microsoft® Excel file designed to help get staff started on creating one-page dashboard reports. A few worthy notes:

- This dashboard generator requires that the metrics to be used in the dashboard have already been defined (perhaps by one of the methods suggested in Chapter 2) and that the data to fuel these metrics have already been collected.

- The user of this dashboard generator needs to be able to work with Microsoft® Excel. But, in general, dashboards do not need to be created in Excel. Other spreadsheet applications with a graphing capability can be used. Presentation software with an imbedded graphing function like Microsoft® PowerPoint is also effective. Even most word processing software can be used.

- The templates provided should be considered a starting point for thinking about how to design a dashboard that meets the needs of the organization in question. Not all of the features or options suggested need to be used, and others not found on the CD-ROM might make more sense.

The dashboard generator consists of three worksheets within a single Excel workbook. The first worksheet contains a set of generic, customizable data entry tables that can be adapted to the user's needs. The next two worksheets contain templates for the two styles of dashboard reports referred to in Chapter 1: a summary (or scorecard) dashboard and a graphic dashboard. To create these dashboards, the user must substitute the organization's real data for the dummy data that appear in the data input worksheet and in the dashboard template worksheets themselves.

Detailed instructions for using the dashboard generator can be found on the CD-ROM.

Conclusion

Board oversight involves more than just reading financial statements, and nonprofit boards don't always know how nor have the opportunity to provide adequate programmatic oversight. Even when board members are familiar with their organization's programs and services, many do *not* know their programs' strengths and weaknesses.

Dashboards have the ability to improve the present way of doing things — resulting in more effective meetings, more thoughtful and informed decision making, and better use of board members' time. They serve as a way of monitoring progress against a strategic plan and annual operating goals. They support evaluation efforts by gathering key performance data on programs and services in the context of a theory of change in real-world outcomes. Ultimately, they give board members needed information that speaks to their governance responsibilities in a compelling and readily understood way.

Creating a dashboard — even just tracking organizational results — isn't easy in the nonprofit sector. But, there are simple ways to start:

- **Less is more.** Resist the temptation to show too many details on every program and activity. Give the board big enough pieces of the picture so that it can get a general idea of the message being conveyed. If the board feels the need to delve deeper into details, that can be pursued in more depth later.

- **Work with readily available data.** Dashboards shouldn't require complicated or expensive data collection. What kind of data are already available to the board? What else is needed and how feasible is it to gather?

- **Carefully pick what goes to the board.** The board shouldn't be burdened with operational information. It only invites micromanagement and misuses the board's valuable time.

The value of the dashboard *design process* goes beyond the reports it generates. By identifying what is important to measure — those few key indicators that reveal the most telling aspects of institutional performance — dashboards can help improve board decision making and ensure institutional success.

SUGGESTED RESOURCES

PUBLICATIONS

BoardSource. *The Source: Twelve Principles of Governance That Power Exceptional Boards*. Washington, DC: BoardSource, 2005. Exceptional boards add significant value to their organizations, making discernible differences in their advance on mission. *The Source* defines governance not as dry, obligatory compliance, but as a creative and collaborative process that supports chief executives, engages board members, and furthers the causes they all serve. It enables nonprofit boards to operate at the highest and best use of their collective capacity. Aspirational in nature, these principles offer chief executives a description of an empowered board that is a strategic asset to be leveraged, and provide board members with a vision of what is possible and a way to add lasting value to the organizations they lead.

Butler, Lawrence. *A Guide to Board Information Systems*. Washington, DC: Association of Governing Boards of Universities and Colleges, 1999. This book discusses ideas and techniques for devising board information systems to inform board members of their key aspects of institutional performance that are mission sensitive and strategic, help define the boundaries between governance and management, and take into account the time constraints of board members. The book discusses the use of dashboard reports, design principles in preparing these and other reports, the value of specificity, and how board members can get up to speed in understanding a common base of information.

Chait, Richard P. *How To Help Your Board Govern More and Manage Less*. Washington, DC: BoardSource, 2003. Is your board managing instead of governing? Understanding this distinction will increase your board's ability to work effectively. Discover how your board can successfully work with staff, and how this dynamic changes as the size of your organization's staff changes. Also included are specific procedures to strengthen your board's capacity to govern.

Connolly, Paul M. *Navigating the Organizational Lifecycle: A Capacity-Building Guide for Nonprofit Leaders*. Washington, DC: BoardSource, 2006. This evergreen resource encourages nonprofit board members and executives to be more proactive and informed about what comes with growth and change. It presents a theory of the evolutionary development of nonprofit organizations, explaining the nonprofit organizational lifecycle model and why it matters; core components of organizational capacity and how they influence an organization's successful development; how a board's composition and responsibilities change at each stage of the lifecycle; how to anticipate future challenges, strengthen capacities, and align lifecycle stages with capacities; and how to obtain funder support for nonprofit organizational development. Don't miss the organizational lifecycle assessment tool available on CD-ROM!

Eckerson, Wayne W. *Performance Dashboards: Measuring, Monitoring, and Managing Your Business*. New York: John Wiley & Sons, 2005. This resource shows how leading companies are using performance dashboards to execute strategy, optimize business processes, and improve performance through the use of case studies and industry research.

Few, Stephen. *Information Dashboard Design: The Effective Visual Communication of Data*. Sebastopol, CA: O'Reilly Media, 2006. Dashboards have become popular in recent years as uniquely powerful tools for communicating important information at a glance. This book will teach the visual design skills needed to create dashboards that communicate clearly, rapidly, and compellingly.

Fischer, Daryl and Lawrence Butler. *Strategic Thinking and Planning: Templates for Trustees*. Washington, DC: Museum Trustee Association, 2004. This resource contains 16 different tools to help museum leaders build an effective strategic plan and regularly monitor progress toward strategic goals.

Flynn, Outi. *Meet Smarter: A Guide to Better Nonprofit Board Meetings*. Washington, DC: BoardSource, 2004. Whether you're new to the boardroom or an old pro, you'll find ready-to-use information in this resource. Based on actual meeting observations, this book will provide you with practical solutions to better meetings, explanation of the legal framework, and process practices that will reinvigorate your board meetings. With a detailed table of contents, this book is a must-have reference guide for nonprofit chief executives, board members, senior staff, and any other participant in key meetings of the board.

Grace, Kay Sprinkel. *The Nonprofit Board's Role in Setting and Advancing the Mission*. Washington, DC: BoardSource, 2003. Is your board supporting and advancing your organization's mission? Learn how board members can actively contribute to the creation of mission as well as communicate the mission and purpose to the community. Discover how your board can partner with organizational staff to implement mission and supporting policies.

Kaplan, Robert S. and David P. Norton. "The Balanced Scorecard: Measures That Drive Performance." *Harvard Business Review*. July 2005. Authors Robert Kaplan and David Norton propose an innovative solution for managers who want a balanced presentation of measures that allow them to view the organization from several perspectives at once.

Measuring Program Outcomes: A Practical Approach. Alexandria, VA: United Way of America, 1996. This resource is a step-by-step manual for health, human service, and youth- and family-serving agencies on specifying program outcomes, developing measurable indicators, identifying data sources and data collection methods, analyzing and reporting findings, and using outcome information. It includes worksheets, examples, and a bibliography on measurement issues and performance indicators.

Murray, Vic. "The State of Evaluation Tools and Systems for Nonprofit Organizations." 2005. www.tess.org/misc/VMSummary.html. This Web article helps the reader determine what an ideal evaluation system would look like.

Presenting: Board Orientation. An Introductory Presentation for Nonprofit Board Members. Washington, DC: BoardSource, 2001. *Presenting: Board Orientation* is a ready-made, customizable, on-screen presentation that can be used as a traditional Microsoft® PowerPoint graphics presentation, as overhead transparency slides, or printed out for handouts. Each slide is accompanied by a set of presentation notes and talking points to guide the discussion. Also included is a 16-page user's guide with suggestions for a board handbook, instructions for customizing the presentation for your board, and tips for a successful board orientation or recruitment session.

Tufte, Edward R. *The Visual Display of Quantitative Information*. Cheshire, CT: Graphics Press, 2001. This classic book on statistical graphics, charts, and tables focuses on the theory and practice in the design of data graphics. The text includes 250 illustrations of the best (and worst) statistical graphics, with detailed analysis of how to display data for precise, effective, quick analysis.

Yankey, John A. and Amy McClellan. *The Nonprofit Board's Role in Planning and Evaluation*. Washington, DC: BoardSource, 2003. Strategic planning and outcome measurement are important issues for every nonprofit board. Learn how your board should be involved in strategic planning and how that plan should link to assessing results. Discover different options for measuring organizational effectiveness and how to analyze both the organization and specific programs. Don't miss the suggestions for dealing with the results of your evaluation.

WEB SITES

http://national.unitedway.org/outcomes/

The United Way of America's Web site provides an Outcomes Measurement Resource Network. Learn more about their outcome measurement program and find additional resources.

www.theoryofchange.org

A Theory of Change is an innovative tool to design and evaluate social change initiatives. By creating a blueprint of the building blocks required to achieve a social change initiative's long-term goal, such as improving a neighborhood's literacy levels or academic achievement, a Theory of Change offers a clear road map to achieve results identifying the preconditions, pathways, and interventions necessary for an initiative's success. On this site, please find: "Guided Example: Project Superwomen." ActKnowledge and the Aspen Institute Roundtable on Comprehensive Community Initiatives, 2003.